TEACH Y
SPANISH

Published by
Sterling Publishers Private Limited

TEACH YOURSELF
SPANISH

VIJAYA VENKATARAMAN
ROSER NOGUERA MAS

A Sterling Paperback

STERLING PAPERBACKS
An imprint of
Sterling Publishers (P) Ltd.
A-59, Okhla Industrial Area, Phase-II,
New Delhi-110020.
Tel: 26387070, 26386209; Fax: 91-11-26383788
E-mail: sterlingpublishers@airtelbroadband.in
ghai@nde.vsnl.net.in
www.sterlingpublishers.com

Teach Yourself Spanish
© 1999, Sterling Publishers (P) Ltd. New Delhi
ISBN 81 207 2172 1
Reprint 2001, 2007

Printed and Published by Sterling Publishers Pvt. Ltd.,
New Delhi-110020.

CONTENTS

UNIT

INTRODUCTION

This book is meant for all those who want to learn Spanish and cannot have the opportunity of a classroom experience. It is directed to travellers and businessmen, who may wish to visit a Spanish speaking country. It seeks to equip the learner to deal with everyday situations like socialising, shopping, eating out, finding accommodation, asking for directions in the street, etc. At the same time, it could also be useful for students doing a course in Spanish. The book cannot substitute a teacher, nor does it pretend to be a manual for teaching/learning Spanish.

As the book is situation-based and is meant for self-study, it is suggested that the learner study the contents carefully before beginning to use the book. The book consists of 15 units – each unit dealing with a different communicative situation. The units are arranged in graded order depending upon the level of difficulty of the learner. The student must begin with Unit 1 and proceed progressively while a traveller requiring specific vocabulary related to a particular situation could go directly to the concerned unit. The last two units (14 and 15) contain elements of advanced grammar and would be useful for those who wish to acquire an intermediate level. The guide to units clearly show the situation dealt with in each unit as well as the grammatical elements and related vocabulary. The chapter on pronunciation follows. Before beginning to study the units, the learner must master the pronunciation rules.

Each unit begins with a set of dialogues in Spanish based on everyday life situations followed by their equivalents in English. The translations are not literal, so the learner must use them only for understanding the dialogues. This is followed by a list of useful phrases for people who want to learn how to use the language in specific situations. This is followed by some topic-based vocabulary. Thereafter, the learner can study the grammatical explanations. In some units, we also include some vocabulary related to their usage with verbs. There are some exercises at the end of each unit for the learner to test his knowledge. Answers can be checked in the key at the end of the book. There are two appendices – one with the conjugation pattern of the regular and irregular verbs and another on nouns. There is also a complete list of useful verbs along with the appendix. At the end of the book, a complete list of vocabulary is given with meanings in Spanish as well as in English.

We would like to thank our friends, María Gil Burmann and Vibha Maurya, for helping us with their suggestions and comments.

Vijaya Venkataraman
Roser Noguera Mas

GUIDE TO UNITS

Possessives Adjectives and Pronouns
Direct Object Pronouns
Coordinations
Relative Pronouns

Vocabulary

Parts of the house
Furniture
Things in the bathroom
Adjectives to describe people and things
Colours

UNIT 3
In the Street

Situation

Asking for directions in the street
Expressing ignorance
Using public transport

Grammar

Prepositions
Prepositions and Verbs
Prepositional Pronouns
Verbal Phrases
Indefinite Adjectives
Double Negatives

Vocabulary

Things on the street
Public buildings, monuments, institutions
At the post office
At the photography shop

UNIT 4
Telling the Time

Situation

Talking of plans, decisions and future actions
Time

Grammar

Reflexive Verbs
Immediate Future (*ir* + *a* + infinitive)
Adjectives to express habituality
Partitive Indefinite Adjectives
The Prepositions *a, de* and *por* with Time

Vocabulary

Expressions and words of daily routine
Expressions with 'ir'
Cardinal and Ordinal Numbers

UNIT 5
Weather

Situation

The weather in different parts of the country
Talking of past actions

Grammar

The verb 'hacer' and 'ser' to describe weather
Impersonal verbs to describe weather
The Present Perfect and the Past Indefinite Tenses
Uses of 'ya', 'todavía (no)'

Vocabulary

Expressions with 'hacer' and 'tener'
Months, days of the week, seasons, cardinal points.
Indicators of time/frequency

UNIT 6
Eating Out

Situation

Ordering in restaurants/cafes
Paying the bill
Recipes

Grammar

The Imperative
Direct and Indirect Object Pronouns

Vocabulary
Food and cooking
Ingredients, utensils and kitchen appliances

UNIT 7
Travelling

Situation
Making enquiries at the airport and railway station
Buying and cancelling tickets
Sightseeing

Grammar
Future Tense

Vocabulary
Travelling by air/ train/ bus/ car
Sightseeing

UNIT 8
Accommodation

Situation
Getting accommodation in a hotel

Grammar
Conditions in requests, orders and invitations

Vocabulary
In the hotel

UNIT 9
At The Bank

Situation
Changing money
Opening a bank account

Vocabulary
Things we need or do in a bank

Vocabulary
Entertainment
Mass media
Activities
Sports

UNIT 13
Health

Situation
Going to the doctor/ dentist/ hospital
Describing symptoms and health

Vocabulary
Hospital,
Medicines
Complaints
Parts of the body

UNIT 14
Troubles

Situation
Asking for help
Reporting loss
Complaining
Apologising

Grammar
Indirect Speech
Passive Voice
The Present and Past Subjunctive, contrast with the Indicative
Compound Tenses

UNIT 15
Expressing Opinions and Exchanging Ideas

Situation
Discussing music, films, politics and fashion
Organising a speech

Grammar
Conditionals
Compound Conditionals
The Past Subjunctive
Temporal Phrases with the Subjunctive

PRONUNCIATION

We have tried to give a clear idea of Spanish pronunciation using the international phonetics and with examples in English. The user may go through the rules very carefully and master the pronunciation following the rules before beginning to study the Units. Pronunciation is acquired through practice and the user may practice the rules along with the examples given to acquire the exact sound. The rules of accent, punctuation and capitalisation are given at the end as additional information.

Vowels

a – *a* as in f*a*ther

e – as *e* in th*ey*, when at the end of a syllable (open syllable)
   as *e* in s*e*t, when a consonant ends the syllable (closed syllable)

i (y) – as *i* in mach*i*ne

o – as *o* in *o*pen, at the end of a syllable (open syllable)
   like *ou* in b*ou*ght, when a consonant ends the syllable (closed syllable)

u – like *u* in r*u*le

y – As the vowel – that is the conjunction y 'and', and at the end of a word such as le*y*, vo*y* – is pronounced like *i*.

Consonants

b	[b], [β]	bomba	At the start of a breath group and after m and n the sound is plosive like the b in book.
		haba	In all other positions it is pronounced such that the lips do not meet.
c ce,ci	[k] [qe, qi]	cama cena cinta	c before a, o or u is pronounced as in can c before e or i is pronounced as in think, in some Latin American areas and in southern Spain it is pronounced [s], like s in sorry.
ch	[tʃ]	chino	ch is pronounced as ch in Chinese
d	[d, ð]	dólar ciudad	At the beginning of a word or after l or n, d, it is pronounced as in dad. In all other positions it is pronounced like th in the.
f	[f]	falda	like f in for.
g	[g, g]	gato toga	g before a, o or u is pronounced as in go, if at the beginning of a word or after n. In other positions the sound is softened.
ge, gi	[xe,xi]	genio gitano	g before e or i is pronounced like, though stronger than kh in Khalid.
h		hacer	h is always silent in Spanish.
j	[x]	jarra	j is pronounced like, though a little stronger than, kh in Khalid.
k	[k]	kilo	like k in kick.
l	[l]	lema	like the English l in love.
ll	[j] [l]	calle	ll is pronounced like lli in million; in some Latin American areas is pronounced like [j] or [l].
m	[m]	mano	like the English m in made.
n	[n]	nada	like the English n in none; but if written before v it is pronounced m [mb] like in enviar
ñ	[h]	niño	ñ is like ny pronounced as in canyon.
p	[p]	palo	like the English p in put, without any aspiration.
qu	[k]	queso	qu is pronounced as k in king.
r, rr	[r, rr]	cantar jarro	r is always pronounced in Spanish, unlike the silent r in dancer. When a word begins with r, it is trilled. rr is always trilled.
s	[s]	quizás	s is usually pronounced as in pass.
t	[t]	patata	like the English t in tame, but without any aspiration.
v	[b, b]	vaca cueva	v is pronounced something like b. At the beginning of a word or after m or n it is pronounced as b in boy. In any other position, the sound is softened.
x	[ks]	examen	like English x in box
y	[j]	yate	y is pronounced like y in yes.
z	[q]	zapatero	z is pronounced as in think, in some Latin American areas and in southern Spain is pronounced [s], like s in sorry.

Diphthongs

a, *e* and *o* are open vowels. *i* (*y*) and u are closed vowels. An open and a closed vowel, or two closed vowels together form a diphthong and hold together as one syllable. These are the diphthongs in Spanish:

ai (ay) – like **I**
vais, hay

au – like **ou** in **out**
causa, autor

ei (ey) – like **ey** in th**ey**
reina, ley

eu – like **eu** in **way** (is a rare sound in English)
deuda

oi (oy) – like **oy** in b**oy**
hoy, oidor

ia – like **ya** in **ya**cht
viajar, secretaria

ie – like **ye** in **ye**ll
pierde, quien

io – like **yo** in **yo**ke
polio, folio

ua – like **wa** in **wa**s
agua

ue – like **we** in **we**nt
puerta, cuesta

uo – like **wo** in **wo**ve
antiguo

ui (y) – like **we**
ruido, muy

Accent

1. Words ending in a consonant (except **n** or **s**) stress the last syllable: can-**tad**, tra-ba-**jar**, i-de-**al**,

2. Words ending in a vowel or in the consonants **n** or **s** stress the penultimate or the next-to-last syllable: cua-**der**-no, se-**ma**-na, **ha**-blan, **u**-nos,

3. Words that do not conform to the above two rules carry a written accent mark over the stressed vowel: **mú**-si-ca, **ár**-bol, can-**tó**, ja-**más**, **fá**-cil, can-ta-**rá**,

4. A diphthong carrying no written accent and composed of an open and a closed vowel stresses the open vowel: gu**a**-pa, cu**es**-ta, pu**e**-de

Punctuation

Punctuation rules are more or less the same as in English except for the following differences:

1. In Spanish, the inverted question mark (¿) and exclamation mark (¡) are used to begin a question and exclamation respectively.
   ¿Hay mucha gente en tu casa?
   ¡Hola! ¿Qué tal?

2. In dialogues, the dash (-) is used instead of quotation marks.

Capitalisation

Unlike English, in Spanish, small letters are used for:

a) Adjectives of nationality
   el vino español, los gorros rusos, el café colombiano

b) Names of languages
   italiano, inglés

c) Names of the days of the week and months
   lunes, domingo, enero, diciembre

d) The pronoun **yo**

THE ALPHABET

A a : a	**N n : ene**
B b : be	**Ñ ñ : eñe**
C c : ce	**O o : o**
Ch ch : che	**P p : pe**
D d : de	**Q q : qu**
E e : e	**R r : erre**
F f : efe	**S s : ese**
G g : ge	**T t : te**
H h : hache	**U u : u**
I i : i	**V v : uve**
J j : jota	**W w : uve doble**
K k : ka	**X x : equis**
L l : ele	**Y y : i griega**
Ll ll : elle	**Z z : zeta**
M m : eme	

Unit 1
MEETINGS AND INTRODUCTIONS

Manuel se encuentra con Ana en la calle y le presenta a su amigo Pedro.

M: ¡Eh, hola!
A: ¡Hombre, Manuel! ¿Qué tal?
M: Mira, este es mi amigo Pedro, es periodista.
P: ¡Hola! Encantado. ¿Cómo te llamas?
A: Ana.
P: ¿De dónde eres?
A: Soy argentina, de Buenos Aires. ¿Y tú?
P: De Bilbao. ¿Y a qué te dedicas?
A: Soy psiquiatra, trabajo en Madrid.
M: Ana está buscando un compañero de piso.
P: ¡Ah, sí!, ¿y dónde vives?
A: En la calle Concepción Arenal, número 3, quinto piso.
P: ¡Qué bien! Yo también estoy buscando piso.
P: ¡Estupendo! ¿Por qué no vienes a verlo?

Ana está con un paciente en el hospital.

P: Buenos días, Señora Alvarez.
A: Hola, buenos días. Usted es ....
P: Jack Long.
A: Ah, sí, ¿cómo se escribe?
P: J-A-C-K-L-O-N-G.
A: ¿Habla español?
P: Un poco.
A: Bien, ... ¿cuántos años tiene?
P: 58.

Manuel meets Ana in the street and introduces her to Pedro.

M: Hey, Hello!
A: Hello, Miguel! How are you?
M: Look, this is my friend Pedro, he is a journalist.
P: Hello! Glad to meet you. What is your name?
A: Ana.
P: Where are you from?
A: I am an Argentinean, from Buenos Aires. And you?
P: I am from Bilbao. And what do you do?
A: I am a psychiatrist. I work in Madrid.
M: Ana is looking for a flat - mate.
P: Oh, really? And where do you live?
A: In Concepción Arenal, number 3, 5th floor.
P: How nice! I am also looking for a flat.
A: Great! Why don't you come and see it?

Ana is with a patient in the hospital.

P: Good Morning, Mrs. Alvarez.
A: Hello, Good Morning! You are…?
P: Jack Long.
A: Oh, yes! How do you spell it?
P: J-A-C-K-L-O-N-G.
A: Do you speak Spanish?
P: A little.
A: OK,… How old are you?
P: 58.

2

USEFUL PHRASES

In all the phrases given below, we give the informal (tú) form followed by the polite (usted) form.

Civilities

¿Qué tal? - How do you do?
¿Cómo estás/ está? - How are you?
Muy bien, ¿y tú/ usted? - Very well, and you?
Gracias - Thank you
Muchas gracias - Thank you very much
De nada - That's all right/ Welcome/ It doesn't matter.
Por favor - Please
¡Perdona/ perdone! - Excuse me
Lo siento - I'm sorry

Small talk about yourself

¿Cómo te llamas/ se llama? - What is your name?
Me llamo ... - My name is ...

¿De dónde eres/ es? - Where do you come from?
Soy de .... - I am from .....

¿Dónde vives/ vive? - Where do you live?
Vivo en (Lima) - I live in (Lima)

¿A qué te dedicas/ se dedica?/ ¿En qué trabajas/ trabaja?/ ¿Qué haces/ hace? - What do you do? /Where do you work?
Trabajo en (una agencia de viajes) - I work in (a travel agency).
Soy (médico) - I am (a doctor)

¿Cuántos años tienes/ tiene? - How old are you?
Tengo ... años - I am ... years old.

Language troubles

¿Hablas/ habla (español)? - Do you speak (Spanish)?
No entiendo (español) - I don't understand (Spanish).
¿Me entiendes/ entiende? - Do you understand me?
(No) te entiendo - I (do not) understand you.

3

¿Puedes/ puede hablar un poco más despacio? - Can you speak a little slower?
¿Puedes/ puede hablar más alto? - Can you speak louder?
¿Puedes/ puede repetir? - Can you repeat?
¿Puedes/ puede traducírmelo? - Can you translate it for me?
¿Cómo se escribe/deletrea? - How do you spell it?
¿Cómo? - a colloquial phrase asking somebody to repeat.

Greetings

Hola - Hello
Buenos días - Good morning
Buenas tardes - Good afternoon
Buenas noches - Good night

Goodbyes

Hasta luego - See you later
Hasta mañana - See you tomorrow
Hasta pronto - See you soon
Adiós - Good bye

VOCABULARY

Work places

(la) agencia de viajes	- travel agency	(la) fábrica	- factory
		(la) oficina	- office
(el) banco	- bank	(la) tienda	- shop
(la) clínica	- clinic	(el) laboratorio	- laboratory
(la) empresa	- company/ firm	(el) taller	- workshop
(el) estudio	- study		

See unit 3 for public institutions and unit 10 for shops.

Nationalities

americano/a	- American	peruano/a	- Peruvian
argentino/a	- Argentinean	venezolano	- Venezuelan
boliviano/a	- Bolivian	mejicano/a	- Mexican
brasileño/a	- Brazilian	español/a	- Spanish
chileno/a	- Chilean	ruso/a	- Russian
colombiano/a	- Colombian	italiano/a	- Italian
cubano/a	- Cuban	inglés/a	- English

4

portugués/a	- Portuguese	indio/a	- Indian
francés/a	- French	chino/a	- Chinese
alemán/a	- German	nepalí	- Nepalese
japonés/a	- Japanese	pakistaní	- Pakistani

Note: The masculine singular form is used for the language spoken.

Professions

abogado	- lawyer	empleado	- employee
agricultor	- farmer	empresario	- manager
ama de casa	- housewife	enfermero	- nurse
arquitecto	- architect	escritor	- writer
azafata	- air-hostess	funcionario	- government employee
cajero	- cashier	panadero	- baker
camarero	- waiter	ingeniero	- engineer
carpintero	- carpenter	médico	- doctor
director	- manager, principal	portero	- concierge
cocinero	- cook	profesor	- professor, teacher
decorador	- interior decorator		

The above forms change according to the gender.

albañil	- mason	electricista	- electrician
artista	- artist	estudiante	- student
cantante	- singer	fontanero	- plumber
cartero	- postman	intérprete	- interpreter
dependiente	- shop-assistant	policía	- policeman
deportista	- sportsman	negociante	- businessman

Note: The above words are used irrespective of the gender and are accompanied by the corresponding article.

See Appendix 1 for feminine endings.

Wishing people

Enhorabuena/ Felicidades - Congratulations/ Best Wishes

¡Feliz cumpleaños! - Happy Birthday

¡Feliz Navidad! - Merry Christmas

¡Felices Fiestas! - Happy Festivities!

¡Que te mejores pronto! - Get well soon!

¡Que tengas buen viaje! - Happy journey!

¡Que te vaya bien todo! - All the best!

¡Que tengas suerte! - Good luck!
¡Que te lo pases bien! - Have a good time!
Bienvenido/a - Welcome

Other Expressions

Sí - Yes
No - No
Vale - OK
Bien - Well, actually
Pues - Well, ...
¡Estupendo! - Great!
(Muchas) gracias - Thank you (very much)
Lo siento (mucho) - I am (very) sorry
Por suerte - Luckily
Por casualidad - By chance
¡Que casualidad! - What a coincidence!

Espero que sí/ no - I hope so/ not
Por si acaso - (Just) in case
Puede que sí/ no - Maybe yes/not
Quizá - Perhaps
Tal vez - Maybe
Eso es - That's right
¿Ah, sí? - Oh, really?

GRAMMAR:

• **Sentence structure**

The order of the sentences in Spanish is Subject + Verb + Object in the case of affirmative statements and questions. The punctuation or intonation differentiates between the two. In the case of negative sentences the 'no' precedes the verb. Often the subject pronoun is not used because the verb forms clearly indicate the subject. The subject pronouns are used only to differentiate, emphasise or clarify.

Examples :
¿Hablas español? - Do you speak Spanish?
Trabajamos en Madrid - We work in Madrid
No hablan inglés - They don't speak English.

- ¿Eres Ana?
- ¿Yo?, ¡no! ¡yo soy Carmen!
Are you Ana?
Me, no! I am Carmen.

- **Personal Pronouns**

The subject pronouns in Spanish are:

	Singular	Plural
First Person	yo	nosotros/as
Second Person	tú	vosotros/as
Third Person	él/ ella/ usted	ellos/ ellas/ ustedes

Usted and Ustedes are the formal forms (singular and plural) of the second person, although they take the third person form of the verb.

Examples:

¿Es usted el señor Sánchez? - Are you Mr.Sanchez?
¿Ustedes viven en Barcelona? - Do you live in Barcelona?

- **Verbs**

There are three conjugation types in Spanish: verbs ending in '-ar', '-er' and '-ir'.

See Appendix-2 for conjugation pattern of regular and irregular verbs

Verbs are of three kinds: transitive, intransitive and reflexive. Transitive verbs are those that require a direct object, intransitive are those that don't require a direct object and reflexive verbs are those that are conjugated along with the corresponding reflexive pronouns. There are also some impersonal verbs, mainly used for describing the weather. *(See Unit 4)*

Examples:

Juan corre - Juan is running. (Intransitive)
Ana come pescado - Ana eats fish. (Transitive)
Me lavo el pelo - I wash my hair. (Reflexive)

• The Present Indicative Tense

Conjugation:

verbs ending in-ar	verbs ending in-er	verbs ending in-ir
hablar	**comer**	**vivir**
habl-**o**	com-**o**	viv-**o**
habl-**as**	com-**es**	viv-**es**
habl-**a**	com-**e**	viv-**e**
habl-**amos**	com-**emos**	viv-**imos**
habl-**áis**	com-**éis**	viv-**ís**
habl-**an**	com-**en**	viv-**en**

Note: For conjugations of irregular verbs see Appendix 2.

The Present Tense in Spanish is used to express actions or situations of the chronological present; habitual actions or to refer to universal facts.

It is also used to express continuing actions, and is more widely used than the Present Continuous Tense in Spanish.

Examples:
¿Dónde vives? - Where do you live?
No trabajo en Bilbao - I don't work in Bilbao.
Los niños juegan en el jardín - The children are playing in the garden.

• Some prepositions

en
vivir + **en** - to live in
trabajar + **en** - to work in

de
ser + **de** - to be from
de also denotes possession and belonging

Examples:
Este libro es de Juan - This is Juan's book.

para - for (in many cases it can be translated as 'to')

When a verb comes after a preposition, it takes the infinitive form:
Comemos para vivir - We eat to live.

- **Ser**

The verb 'SER' is used to express nationality/place of origin and profession.

See Appendix 2 for conjugation

Ser + de + place of origin:

Examples:
Soy de India - I am from India.
Somos de Inglaterra - We are from England.

Ser + nationality or profession:

Examples:
Soy mejicano - I am Mexican.
Ana es argentina - Ana is Argentinean.
Carlos y Pedro son estudiantes - Carlos and Pedro are students.
¿Eres psicóloga? - Are you a psychologist?

- **The Present Continuous Tense**

The Present Continuous tense is used to describe actions taking place at the time of speaking. It does not have as generalised a usage as in English.

It is formed with the present tense of the verb **estar + present participle** (formed by adding - **ando** to -*ar* ending verbs and -**iendo** to -*er/-ir* ending verbs).

estoy			
estás			
está	+	habl	- **ando**
estamos		com	- **iendo**
estáis		escrib	- **iendo**
están			

Irregular Gerunds:
Verbs ending in -*eer* or -*aer* take a *y* in the gerund form. Here are some examples.

creer	-	creyendo
leer	-	leyendo
oír	-	oyendo
traer	-	trayendo
ir	-	yendo

9

Some other verbs which have another kind of irregularity have the following forms:

decir - diciendo
venir - viniendo
dormir - durmiendo
pedir - pidiendo
sentir - sintiendo
servir - sirviendo

Examples:
¿Qué haces?
Estoy leyendo un libro.
What are you doing?
I am reading a book.

• **Nouns**

All nouns in Spanish are masculine or feminine.
el coche, el árbol, la casa, la manzana
Animate nouns have two forms - masculine and feminine - which may be the same or different.

Examples:
el perro   - la perra
el estudiante - la estudiante
el padre   - la madre

Nouns are singular or plural. The plural is formed by adding -s when the noun ends in a vowel and -es when the noun ends in a consonant. When the noun ends in -z the plural is formed by adding -ces.

Examples:
el lápiz - los lápices
la profesora - las profesoras

See Appendix 1 for detailed list of nouns, their gender and number

10

- **Articles**

There are two kinds of articles: definite and indefinite.

	Singular		Plural	
	Masculine	Feminine	Masculine	Feminine
Definite	el	la	los	las
Indefinite	un	una	unos	unas

When the prepositions 'a' or 'de' are followed by the singular, masculine definite article, they take the following form:
a+ el = al
de + el = del

Demonstrative pronouns and adjectives:

Singular		Plural	
Masculine	Feminine	Masculine	Feminine
este	esta	estos	estas
ese	esas	esos	esas
aquel	aquella	aquellos	aquellas

These are used as pronouns as well as adjectives.

Examples:
Este coche es grande - This car is big.
- ¿Quién es aquella?
- Es Lucía.
Who is that girl?
She is Lucía.

- **In Spanish nouns, articles and adjectives agree in number and gender.**

Examples:
Este perro es malo - This dog is bad.
Los niños son buenos - The children are good.
La profesora es simpática - The teacher is kind.
Estas chicas son inteligentes - These girls are intelligent.

- **Interrogative particles**

¿**Cómo** se escribe? - How do you write it?
¿**Qué** haces? - What do you do?

11

¿**Dónde** vives? - Where do you live?
¿**Por qué** estudias español? - Why do you study Spanish?
¿**Quién/ -es** es/son ella/as? - Who is/are she/they?
¿**Cuándo** vienes a mi casa? - When will you come to my house?
¿**Cuál/-es** prefieres? - Which one/ones do you prefer?
¿**Cuánto/ -a/ -os -as**? - How many/how much (in the case of uncountable nouns) coins/money do you have?
¿**Cuánto cuesta?** - How much does it cost?

All these particles can be used with **a, de, con, para, contra, etc.** when the verb that follows requires any of these prepositions:

¿**A quién** buscas? - Whom are you looking for?
¿**Para quién** es esto? - Whom is it for?
¿**De qué** hablan? - What are they talking about?
¿**Contra quién** luchan? - Whom are they fighting against?

¿**Adónde** vas? - Where are you going to?

¿**Por dónde** pasa este autobús? - Where does this bus pass?

*Note that **adónde** is written as one word and is used with verbs of movement. In all other cases, the preposition corresponding to the verb is used.*

Exercises

1. Fill in the blanks with the correct form of the verb *ser*.
a) Juan ..... cubano.
b) Nosotros ..... arquitectos.
c) Ella ...... psicóloga.
d) Carmen y Juan .... estudiantes de alemán.
e) Tú ..... argentino.
f) Ustedes .... de Barcelona.
g) (Yo) ...... Jaime.

2. Choose one word from each box and make sentences according to the rules of concordance between the different elements:

Este	chica	tiene	español
Ø	Alberto	beben	blancos
Las	niño	viven	cerveza
Aquella	mujeres	habla	francesa
Los	Pablo y yo	son	en Madrid
Esos	hombres	es	a baloncesto
Ø	gatos	jugamos	25 años

3. Fill in the banks with the correct form of the verb:
a) ¿Cómo .... (LLAMARSE, tú)?
b) Juan y Vicente .... (TRABAJAR) en una fábrica de coches.
c) Mis hijas .... (ESTAR + ESTUDIAR in gerund) en una universidad privada.
d) Luis y yo .... (IR) a París de vacaciones.
e) Carmen .... (HACER) los deberes.
f) Vosotros no .... (HABLAR) árabe ¿verdad?.
g Yo .... (JUGAR) a fútbol muy bien.

4. Translate the following sentences into Spanish:
a) Marta is from Bilbao. She works in Madrid.
b) Do you live in Delhi?
c) The children are not playing in the garden.

13

Unit 2
SOCIALISING

Pedro va a ver el piso y decide compartirlo con Ana.

Pedro : Hola, ¿qué tal?

Ana : Hola, bienvenido a casa.

P: ¡Huy! ¡Qué agradable!

A: Sí, no es un piso muy grande pero es tranquilo. Ven, te lo enseño. Aquí está el salón. Hay tres dormitorios y dos cuartos de baño. La cocina está al final de este pasillo. También hay un balcón grande y una terraza.

P: ¿Tienes teléfono?

A: Sí, el número es 5 23 42 99.

P: Vale. Si te parece bien puedo venir el lunes con mis cosas.

A: De acuerdo. Mira, enfrente hay un supermercado. Al otro lado de la calle hay un estanco para comprar el periódico, tabaco, etc. Detrás, hay un cine donde ponen películas extranjeras subtituladas.

P: ¡Qué interesante!

David un amigo de Ana llega en este momento.

Ding dong...

A : ¿Quién es?

D: David.

A: ¡Hola, David! Pasa.

D: Hola.

A: Este es Pedro, mi nuevo compañero de piso. David es periodista, trabaja en *La Vanguardia*.

D: Encantado.

A: ¿Quieres tomar algo?

D: Pues, bien. Una cerveza.

A: ¿Y tú, Pedro?

P: Yo también.

14

Ana habla por teléfono con su amiga Carmen:

Rrrriiing....

C: ¿Dígame?

A: Hola, soy Ana. Te llamo para decirte que no voy a tu casa esta tarde.

C: ¿Por qué? ¿Qué pasa?

A: Es que hoy viene mi amigo Roberto de Buenos Aires.

C: ¡Ah!, ¿es el de la foto que tienes en tu habitación?

A: Sí, el alto y moreno.

C: Tiene bigote, ¿no?

A: Sí, tiene bigote y barba, es muy simpático.

Pedro goes to see the flat and decides to share it with Ana.

J: Hello! How do you do?

A: Hello! Welcome.

P: Wow, it's very nice.

A: Yes, the flat is not very big but it is very quiet. Come, I'll show it to you. Here is the drawing room. There are three bedrooms and two bathrooms. The kitchen is at the end of the corridor. There is also a big balcony and a terrace.

J: Do you have a telephone?

A: Yes, the number is 5 23 42 99.

J: OK. If it is fine with you I can come with my things on Monday.

A: That's all right. Look, there is a supermarket in front of the flat. On the other side of the street, there is a newspaper stand where you can buy newspaper, cigarettes etc. Behind, there is a theatre where they show foreign films with subtitles.

J: How interesting!

David, Ana's friend pays a visit just then.

Ding Dong...

A: Who's there?

D: David.

A: Hello, David! Come in.

D: Hello.

A: This is Pedro, my new flatmate. David is a journalist, working for *La Vanguardia*.

D: Pleased to meet you.

A: Would you like to drink something?

D: Well, OK. A beer.

A: And you, Pedro?

P: Me too.

Ana is speaking to her friend, Carmen, on the telephone:

Rriiiing…..

C: Hello!

A: Hello, I am Ana. I am calling to tell you that I can't go to your house this evening.

C: Why, what's the matter?

A: It's just that my friend Roberto is coming from Buenos Aires today.

C: Ah, is he the one who's in the photograph in your room?

A: Yes, he is tall and dark.

C: Doesn't he have a moustache?

A: Yes, he has a moustache and beard, he is very nice.

USEFUL PHRASES

Introducing somebody

Te presento a (Ana), Esta es (Ana), Este es (Pedro)- This is (Ana)

Encantado/a- Pleased to meet you

Toma, aquí tienes mi tarjeta- Here is my card

Si me necesitas ya sabes donde estoy- If you need something, get in touch

Offering your guests a drink/ something to eat

¿Quieres tomar algo? - Would you like something?

Si, un café/ una cerveza/ etc. - Yes, a coffee/ a beer/ etc.

No, gracias - No, thank you

¿Te apetece (un café)? - Do you feel like having (coffee)?

Si, vale/ gracias - Yes, OK/ thank you

No, gracias - No, thank you

¿Quieres comer algo? - Do you want something to eat?

(The answer to the above will be in the negative)

¿Por qué no te quedas para comer/cenar? - Why don´t you stay for lunch/dinner?

(This is used only when it is lunch/dinner time)

16

On the telephone

Dígame - Hello
¿Puedo hablar con (Ana)?- Can I talk to (Ana)?
¿Puede pasarme con el Señor Saldaña, por favor? -
Can I talk to Mr. Saldaña, please?

No cuelgues - Don't hang up.
Sí, ahora te lo paso - Yes, I'll just call him.
No está - He/She isn't there.

Ahora se pone - He/She'll attend you in a moment
Hable más alto, por favor - Please speak loudly
No le oigo - I can't hear you
¿Con quién hablo? - Whom am I speaking to?
¿Es el 2352037? - Is it 2352037?
Se ha equivocado - It's a wrong number.
¿De parte de quién? - Who is calling?
Se oye muy mal - The line is not clear
¿Puedo dejar un mensaje? - Can I leave a message?
¿Quiere dejar un mensaje? - Would you like to leave a message?
Te llamo más tarde - I will call you later
¿Puedes llamarle esta noche? - Can you call her/him back at night?

Tarjeta de teléfono	-	telephone card
Número de teléfono	-	telephone number
Llamar por teléfono	-	to call up
Hablar por teléfono	-	to speak on telephone
Contestar	-	to answer

Partes de la casa - parts of the house

(el) aseo	- toilet	(el) pasillo	- passage, corridor
(el) balcón	- balcony	(la) puerta	- door
(la) cocina	- kitchen	(el) sala de	- living room
(el) comedor	- dining room	estar	
(el/los) cuarto(s)	- bathroom	(el) salón	- drawing room
de baño		(la) terraza	- terrace
(el) dormitorio	- bedroom	(la) ventana	- window
(la) habitación	- room		

Muebles y cosas de la casa - furniture and household things

(el) colchón	- mattress	(la) silla	- chair
(la) cama	- bed	(el) sillón	- armchair
(la) cortina	- curtain	(el) sofá	- sofa
(la) alfombra	- carpet	(el) ventilador	- fan
(el) armario	- cupboard	(el) téléfono	- telephone
(la) estantería	- shelf	(el) enchufe	- plug
(el) cuadro	- painting	(el) televisor	- television
(la) lámpara	- lamp	(la) antena	- antenna
(la) mesa	- table	(las)escaleras	- stairs
(la) sábana	- bedsheet	(el) ascensor	- lift

Cosas del baño - things in the bathroom

(la) bañera	- bathtub	(el) jabón	- soap
(el) cepillo	- brush	(la) maquinilla de afeitar	- shaving razor
(el) cepillo de dientes	- toothbrush	(la) espuma de afeitar	- shaving cream
(el) champú	- shampoo		
(la) crema	- cream	(el) papel higiénico	- toilet paper
(la) compresa	- sanitary towel		
(el) desodorante	- deodorant	(la) pasta de dientes	- toothpaste
(el) detergente	- detergent		
(la) ducha	- shower	(el) peine	- comb
(el) espejo	- mirror	(el) perfume	- perfume
(la) esponja	- sponge	(las)tijeras	- scissors
(el) gel	- gel	(la) toalla	- towel

GRAMMAR

More rules about verbs

- When the main verb is followed by a complimentary one the latter takes the infinitive form.

Examples:

Puedo ir en coche - I can go by car.

Queremos comer pescado - We want to eat fish.

Carmen quiere ver una película - Carmen wants to see a film.

- When a person is the direct object of a sentence, the verb is followed by the preposition **a**.

Examples:
Veo a Juan.
Buscamos a nuestro profesor.

- The verb **estar** is used to
a) denote the geographical location of a place or city

Example:
Madrid está en España - Madrid is in Spain.

b) to tell about the location of an object/person.

Examples:
Estoy en el bar - I am in the bar.
El cine está enfrente de mi casa - The cinema is in front of my house.

c) with a predicate adjective to express temporary quality or feelings/moods

Examples:
Juan está triste - Juan is sad.
Carmen y Alfonso están contentos - Carmen and Alfonso are happy.

Elements which are used with the verb 'estar'

a la derecha (de)	- to the right (of)	encima (de)	- above
		enfrente (de)	- in front of
a la izquierda (de)	- to the left (of)	lejos (de)	- far from
		sobre	- on
al final (de)	- at the end of	entre	- between
al lado (de)	- beside	en	- in
cerca (de)	- near to	dentro (de)	- inside
delante (de)	- in front of	aquí	- here
detrás (de)	- behind	ahí/ allí	- there

Adjectives expressing moods, feelings or state - used with 'estar'

contento/ feliz	- happy	enfermo	- sick
triste	- sad	nervioso	- nervous
serio	- serious	tranquilo	- calm
débil	- weak	ocupado	- busy
borracho	- drunk	preocupado	- worried
cansado	- tired	satisfecho	- satisfied

lleno	- full	limpio	- clean
vacío	- empty	sucio	- dirty

* **Hay** is used for 'there is' and 'there are'. It is not used with definite articles.

Examples :

Hay dos dormitorios en mi casa - There are two bedrooms in my house.

Hay un estanco en la calle - There is a news-stand in the street.

* The verb **ser** is used with adjectives to express inherent or permanent qualities. It is also used to describe things or people.

Examples:

Description of things:

La casa es grande - The house is big.

Este libro es verde - This book is green

Description of people:

Ser + adjectives listed below

Examples:

Juan es alto y gordo.

Ana es alta y morena.

Mis hermanos son buenos.

Tener +

(los) ojos claros (light eyes)

(los) ojos oscuros (dark eyes)

35 años (is 35 years old)

Tener or *llevar* +

bigote (moustache)

barba (beard)

(el) pelo largo (long hair)

(el) pelo corto (short hair)

(el) pelo liso (straight hair)

(el) pelo rizado (curly hair)

Examples:

Mi padre lleva el pelo largo - My father has long hair

Mi amiga tiene pelo rizado - My friend has curly hair

Llevar can also be used to describe somebody's clothes.

Elisa lleva un abrigo muy caro - Elisa is wearing a very expensive coat.

Colours

blanco	- white	rosa	- pink
negro	- black	verde	- green
gris	- grey	azul	- blue
marrón	- brown	violeta	- violet
amarillo	- yellow	claro	- light
naranja	- orange	oscuro	- dark
rojo	- red		

Adjetives to describe people physical attributes

alto	- tall	grande	- big
bajo	- short	pequeño	- small
gordo	- fat	menudo	- small-framed
delgado	- thin	moreno	- dark haired
flaco	- skinny	rubio	- blonde
guapo	- beautiful	pelirrojo	- red-haired
feo	- ugly	pecoso	- freckled

Characteristics of people

aburrido	- boring	celoso	- jealous
divertido	- funny (with a good sense of humour)	envidioso	- envious
		grosero	- rude, indecent
interesante	- interesting	inteligente	- intelligent
serio	- serious	tonto	- stupid
amable	- kind	despistado	- absentminded
simpático	- nice	torpe	- clumsy
antipático	- unkind	generoso	- generous
bueno	- good	tacaño	- miserly
malo	- bad		

Civil status

casado	- married	soltero	- unmarried
divorciado	- divorced	viudo	- widower

Age

niño	- child	adulto	- adult
joven	- young	anciano/a	- old man/woman
		mayor	- old, elderly

Adjectives to describe things

aburrido	- boring	extraño	- strange
interesante	- interesting	raro	- strange
antiguo	- old/ ancient	grande	- big
moderno	- modern	pequeño	- small
nuevo	- new	pesado	- heavy
viejo	- old	ligero	- light
bonito	- beautiful	redondo	- round
feo	- ugly	triangular	- triangular
cómodo	- comfortable	cuadrado	- square
incómodo	- uncomfortable	ovalado	- oval
estupendo	- fantastic		

Adjectives

Adjectives can be used with the verbs 'ser' and 'estar'. They must agree in number and gender with the noun.

Examples:
Esas casas son blancas - Those houses are white.
El niño está enfermo - The child is ill.
La enfermera está cansada - The nurse is tired.
Estos coches son nuevos - These cars are new.

• Adverbs

Adverbs can be formed by adding **-mente** to the feminine forms of adjectives or to those ending in consonants or **-e.**

Examples:
cordial - cordialmente
lenta - lentamente
fuerte - fuertemente

Bueno/malo are adjectives and **bien/mal** are adverbs.
Examples:
Este restaurante es bueno/malo - This restaurant is good/bad.
Andrés trabaja bien/mal.- Andres works well/badly.

Muy - very is a qualifier and can be used with adverbs like *bien, mal,* etc. as well as with adjectives like *grande, inteligente,* etc. When used with adjectives it can be used with either **ser** or **estar**. Ana y Mario son *muy* inteligentes - Ana and Mario are very intelligent.

Bastante - quite as a qualifier is used with adjectives
El piso es *bastante* grande - The flat is quite big.

Mucho - a lot as a quantifier is used with verbs:
José habla *mucho.*- Jose talks a lot.

Poco - a little also as a quantifier is used with verbs
Carlos habla *poco* - Carlos speaks little.

- **Possessive Adjectives**

Possessive is expressed by using the possessive pronouns or the preposition *de:*
article + noun + de + subject.

Examples:
La casa de Juan es grande - Juan's house is big.
Aquel chico es el hermano de Leví - That boy is Levi's brother.

Note : In Spanish, the appostrophe is <u>not</u> used to to indicate possession.

Possessive adjectives agree in number in all the forms and in gender only in the the 1st and 2nd person plural forms with the noun possessed.

mi(s) - my
tu (s) - your
su (s) - his/her
nuestro/a (s) - our
vuestro/a (s) - your
su (s) - their

Examples:
Mis libros están sobre la mesa - My books are on the table.
Nuestras llaves están debajo de la silla - Our keys are under the chair.
¿Dónde está **vuestro** coche?- Where is your car?

Possessive Pronouns

mío, mía/ míos, mías - mine
tuyo, tuya, tuyos, tuyas - yours

suyo, suya, suyos, suyas - his/hers
nuestro, nuestra, nuestros, nuestras - ours
vuestro, vuestra, vuestros, vuestras - yours
suyo, suya, suyos, suyas - theirs

Possessive pronouns substitute the noun and are used with the verb. When used with the corresponding article they substitute the subject noun.

Examples:
Esta casa es nuestra - This house is ours.
Estos cuadros son míos - These paintings are mine.

El mío (mi libro) está sobre la mesa - Mine (my book) is on the table.
Las suyas (sus camisetas) están sucias - Hers (her T-shirts) are dirty.

- **Direct object pronouns**

Direct object pronouns replace direct objects. Here we explain the third person singular and plural forms.

For a more detailed explanation of the position of Indirect and Direct Object pronouns see Unit 5

In the Present Indicative Tense, the Object Pronoun is placed before the conjugated verb and if the verb is in the Infinitive form, it is placed after it.

	Singular	**Plural**
Masculine	lo	los
Feminine	la	las

Examples:
Isabel tiene una bicicleta - Isabel has a bicycle.
Isabel la tiene - Isabel has it.
Veo a los alumnos en el jardín - I see the students in the garden.
Los veo en el jardín - I see them in the garden.
Voy a ver una película esta tarde - I am going to see a film this evening.
Voy a verla esta tarde - I am going to see it this evening.

24

- **Coordinations**

y - and

When *y* comes before a word beginning with *i* or *hi* it becomes *e*.

Examples:

Lorenzo e Isabel viven en Madrid.

Juan enseña geografía e historia en el instituto.

o - or

When *o* comes before a word beginning with *o* or *ho* it becomes *u*.

Example:

Hay siete u ocho personas en la sala.

ni - neither/ nor

Example:

No tengo ni café ni té.

pero - but

Example:

Juan es muy inteligente *pero* no estudia.

sino is used instead of **pero** when the verb is the same.

sino que is used when two different verbs are used.

Example:

No trabajo en el colegio *sino* en la universidad.

José Luis no **quiere** hacer una película. José Luis **va a estudiar** cine.

The above two sentences can be joined as follows:

José Luis no quiere hacer una película *sino que* va a estudiar cine.

- **Relative Phrases: que/ donde/ quien**

que - that
quien - whose
donde - where

que	Manuel es aquel chico *que* tiene el pelo largo. El río *que* pasa por Delhi es el Yamuna.
donde	La cuidad *donde* vivo es muy grande. La ciudad *de donde* vengo está lejos.
quien	El hombre *con quien* hablo es el padre de Luis. Miguel es el chico *al que/ a quien* veo todos los días.

Note: All the relative pronouns can be used with or without prepositions but quien is always preceded by either de, a, con, contra, etc.

Exercises

1. Use the correct form of the verb *ser*, *estar* or *hay* to fill in the blanks:
a) El libro ..... verde.
b) Nuestras profesoras ...... cansadas.
c) .... un cine en mi barrio.
d) ¿Quiénes..... aquellos hombres?
e) Ellos ...... en el bar.

2. Match the columns

COLUMN A	COLUMN B
Las casas	nuevo
Los médicos	grandes
La mujer	buenos
El reloj	alta y guapa
Los edificios	rojas
El vestido	modernos
Las flores	amarilla
La camisa	sucio

3. Fill in the blanks with *que, quien, donde, bastante, muchas, muy, pocas, pero*.
a) En el bar .... siempre quedamos hay .... mesas.
b) Hay .... frutas .... no me gustan: los plátanos, las naranjas, la piña...
c) El chico de .... te hablo siempre, es aquel moreno.
d) Alicia me parece .... guapa .... no es muy simpática.

4. Translate the following sentences into Spanish:
a) Are the keys on the table?
b) Santa Fe Hospital is next to Ana's clinic. It is big and very good.
c) My father is tall and fat. He has a beard. Today he is wearing a black coat and a checked jacket.
d) There are many books on my table.

Unit 3
IN THE STREET

Pedro pregunta por un supermercado en la calle.

P: Perdone, ¿hay un supermercado cerca?
X: Sí, hay uno en la calle Luna.
P: ¿Y cómo se va?
X: Mire, siga todo recto, coja la primera calle a la izquierda y cruce la plaza. Allí está.
P: Muchas gracias.
X; De nada.

Juan quiere ir a la universidad y pregunta a Ana y a Pedro.

J: Ana, ¿cómo se va a la universidad?
A: Lo siento, pero no lo sé.
J: Oye, Pedro ¿sabes cómo podemos ir a la universidad?
Pedro: Pues, coged el autobús 44 y bajad en la última parada. Llegáis a Moncloa y de allí podéis ir andando. Seguid todo recto hasta el final de la calle, torced a la derecha y allí enfrente está la Facultad de Biología.
J: Vale, gracias.

Pedro asks for a supermarket on the street:.

J: Excuse me, is there a supermarket here?
X: Yes, there is one in Luna Street.
J: How does one go there?
X: Look, go straight, and take the first street to the left and cross the square. It's right there.
J: Thanks a lot.
X: Welcome.

Juan wants to go to the University. He asks Ana and Pedro for directions.

J: Ana, how does one go to the University?

A: I'm sorry, but I don't know.

J: Listen, Pedro, do you know how we can get to the University?

Pedro: Well, you can catch bus no. 44 and get off at the last stop. You reach Moncloa and you can walk from there. Follow the road right to the end. Then, turn to the right and there, right in front, is the Faculty of Biology.

J: Fine, thanks.

USEFUL PHRASES

Around Town

¿Puedo ayudarle?- May I help you?

¿Sabe(s) si hay un banco por aquí?- Do you know if there is a bank here?

¿Puede(s) decirme cómo se va a (la plaza Castilla)?- Could you tell me how to go to (Plaza Castilla)?

¿Dónde está (el mercado)?- Where is (the market)?

Estoy buscando (una farmacia) - I'm looking for (a chemist shop)

¿Está muy lejos de aquí?- Is it far from here?

¿Queda muy lejos (el banco)?- How far is (the bank)?

¿Cuántos kilómetros hay de (Valencia) a (Alicante)?- How many kilometres is it from (Valencia) to (Alicante)?

¿Qué calle es esta?- What street is this?

¿Cómo se va a (la universidad)? How does one go to (the University)?

¿Cómo voy a (la calle Marqués de Campo)?- How do I go to (Marqués de Campo Street)?

¿Cuándo abren?- When do they open?

¿Cuándo cierran?- When do they close?

Lo siento, no lo sé- I'm sorry, I don't know.

Lo siento, no soy de aquí- I'm sorry. I don't live here.

Siga/sigue recto- Go straight

Coja/coge (la primera calle) - Take (the first street)

Tuerza/tuerce a (la derecha) - Turn to (the right)

Gire/a a (la izquierda) - Take a turn to (the left)

¿Ve (aquel edificio rojo)?- Can you see (that red building)?
Allí verá (un banco)- There you will see (a bank).
Allí hay (una plaza)- There is (a square) there.

Getting a bus or metro in the city
¿Dónde hay una boca de metro? - How do I get to the metro?
¿Me puede dar un plano del metro? - Can you give me a metro map?

¿Dónde está la parada de autobuses? - Where is the bus-stop?
¿Cómo puedo llegar al (Museo del Prado)? - How can I get to the Prado Museum?

Getting a taxi
¿Me puede llevar a esta dirección? - Can you take me to this address?
Lléveme a ......, por favor - Please take me to ......
¿Cuánto costará? - How much will it be?

See Unit 8 for related vocabulary

En el estanco - At the News Stand (Newsagent/Tobacconist)

Quería el peródico de hoy - I wanted today's newspaper.
¿Tienen periódicos (en inglés)? - Do you have (English) newspapers?
¿Me puede dar un paquete de (Fortuna)? - Can you give me a packet of (Fortuna)?

(el) chicle	- chewing gum
(la) chocolatina	- chocolate bar
(el) tabaco	- tobacco
(el) paquete de cigarrillos	- packet of cigarettes
(la) guía de (Madrid)	- guidebook of (Madrid)
(el) mapa de (Barcelona)	- map of (Barcelona)
(el) mapa de carreteras	- road map
(el) mechero	- lighter
(las) cerillas	- matches
(el) periódico	- newspaper
(la) revista	- magazine

(el) papel	-	paper
(el) bolígrafo	-	pen
(la) tarjeta de teléfono	-	telephone card

En la oficina de Correos - At the Post Office

Esta carta es para (Caracas) - This letter is for (Caracas).

¿Cuánto cuesta enviar esta carta a (México)? - How much does it cost to send this letter to (Mexico)?

Deme un sello para carta/ postal - Give me a stamp for a letter/ postcard.

¿Me da 3 sellos de 35 pesetas? - I want three 35 pesetas stamps, please.

¿Me da un recibo? - Can you give me a receipt, please.

Quiero enviar esta carta por correo certificado - I want to register this letter.

¿Hay correo para (el Señor Mestre)? - Have you received any mail for (Mr. Mestre)?

Por avión- by airmail

(el) sobre	-	envelope
(el) buzón	-	letterbox
(el) correo	-	mail
(el) paquete	-	packet, parcel
(la) postal	-	postcard
(la) carta certificada	-	registered letter
(el) sello	-	stamp
(el) telegrama	-	telegram

En una tienda de fotos - At the Photography Shop

Quería un carrete para esta cámara - I'd like a film for this camera.

Quería revelar este carrete - I'd like this film developed.

¿Podría ampliar esta, por favor? - Can you enlarge this, please?

¿Cuánto cuesta el revelado de (36) fotos? - How much do (36) exposures cost?

¿Cuándo estarán las fotos? - When will the photos be ready?

Quería recoger mis fotos - I'd like to pick up my photos.

Aquí tiene el recibo - Here is the receipt.

(las) pilas	- battery	(el) objetivo	- lens
24/36 fotos	- 24/36 exposures	(el) filtro	- filter
blanco y negro	- black and white	(el) flash	- flash
color	- color		

VOCABULARY

Things on the street

(la) farola	- lamppost	(la) avenida	- avenue
(la) esquina	- corner	(la) calle	- street
(la) fuente	- fountain	(el) paseo	- avenue
(la) acera	- pavement	(la) plaza	- square
(el) semáforo	- traffic light	(el) centro de la ciudad	- city centre
(la) señal de tráfico	- traffic sign		

Public buildings, mounuments and instituitions

(el) ayuntamiento	- town hall	(el) museo	- museum
(la) biblioteca	- library	(el) palacio	- palace
(el) colegio	- school	(el) parque	- park
(la) universidad	- university	(los) bomberos	- fire brigade
correos	- post office	(la) policía	- police
(el) hospital	- hospital	(la) iglesia	- church
(el) mercado	- market	(la) mezquita	- mosque
(la) oficina de turismo	- tourism office	(la) sinagoga	- synagogue
		(el) templo	- temple

See unit 10 for shop's names
See unit 8 for transport

GRAMMAR

• **Prepositions**

por - through, for, by
Este tren pasa *por* Agra - This train goes through Agra.
Mandamos las cartas *por* correo - We send the letters by post.
Paseamos *por* el parque cuando tenemos tiempo - We walk through the park when we have time.

sin - without
Ana va a clase *sin* libros - Ana goes to class without her books.

con - with
Voy al cine *con* Marta - I go to the cinema with Marta.

sobre - on, about
Habla *sobre* un tema muy interesante - He speaks about a very interesting topic.

When a verb comes after a preposition, it takes the infinitive form:
Comemos para vivir. - We eat to live.

- **Prespositional Pronouns**

Prepositions are followed by prepositional pronouns. These are:
mí
ti
él/ella/ud.
nosotros
vosotros
ellos/ellas/uds.

But with **'con', conmigo, contigo** is used with the 1st and 2nd person singular and plural respectively. In the other forms the prepositional pronouns are used. **Consigo** is used for the third person if the subject coincides with the object.
Examples:
Este libro es para mí - This book is for me.
Estoy pensando en ti - I am thinking of you.
Está contenta consigo misma. - She is happy with herself.

- **Prepositions and verbs**

ir a - to go to
Todos los días *voy a* la universidad - Everyday I go to the University.

llegar a - to reach
El avión *llega a* las 5 - The flight reaches at 5 o'clock.

Pasear por - to take a walk
Todos los lunes *paseamos por* el parque - Every Monday, we walk in the park.

Pasar por - to go through
Este autobús *pasa por* Zaragoza - This bus passes through Zaragoza.

Parar en - to stop at
Ese tren no *para en* todas las estaciones - That train does not stop at all the stations.

Entrar en - to enter
El perro no *entra en* casa - The dog does not enter the house.

Volver de - to return from
¿Cuándo *vuelves de* El Cairo? - When do you return from Cairo?

Salir de - to leave (from)
Salgo de clase a la 1 - I leave class at 1 o'clock.

Venir de - to come from
¿*De dónde* vienes? - Where do you come from?

Preguntar por - to ask about, to enquire
Juan *pregunta por* una farmacia en la calle - Juan is asking about a chemist shop in the street.

Quedar con - to fix an appointment or meeting with somebody.
Quedamos el sábado por la tarde a las ocho con unos amigos - We'll meet some friends at eight on Saturday.

Preocuparse por - to be worried about (someone, something)
Marisa *se preocupa* mucho *por* su hija - Marisa is very worried about her daughter.

Pensar en algo/alguien - to think of/about someone/something
Estoy *pensando en* mi examen de conducir - I am thinking of my driving exam.

Despedirse de - to say goodbye to
Nos *hemos despedido de* Vicente este fin de semana - We said goodbye to Vicente this weekend.

Encontrarse con - to meet (by chance or suddenly)
Esta mañana *me he encontrado con* Chandra en el metro - This morning I met Chandra in the metro.

- **Verbal Phrases**

Verbal Phrases are expressions consisting of a verb followed by an infinitive, participle or the gerund of another verb, sometimes introduced by prepositions. Below we give examples of those that are more commonly used.

Acabar de - to just finish
Acabo de comer - I've just eaten.

Dejar de - to give up
Pilar va a *dejar de* estudiar en abril - Pilar is going to give up her studies in April.

Parar de - to stop
Ha parado de llover - It has stopped raining.

Tener que + (ir) - to have (to go)
Tengo que visitar a mi abuela - I have to visit my grandmother.

Ir a - to be going to
Voy a comer - I am going to eat.
See Unit 4 for a more detailed explanation of this expression.

Ir + gerund
Vivo cerca de la oficina *y voy andando* - I live near the office and I go walking.
This is sometimes used with the expression *poco a poco* to give the idea of something gradually developing
Voy pintando la casa poco a poco - I am painting the house little by little.

Estar a punto de - to be on the point of
Estoy a punto de acabar - I am almost finishing.

Empezar a - to begin to
Ponerse a - to begin to
Empiezo a entender las cosas - I am beginning to understand things.
Voy a *ponerme* a estudiar el inglés - I am going to begin to study English.

Llevar + participle / gerund
Llevamos casados más de diez años - We have been married more than ten years.
Llevo tres años *estudiando* español - I've been studying Spanish for three years.

Seguir /continuar + gerund - to continue (reading, working, etc.)
Sigo trabajando en la misma oficina - I am still working in the same office.

• **Indefinite Adjectives**

Cierto/a/ os/ as   - certain
This is used with countable nouns as a determinant.

Example:
Por la noche, oigo ciertos ruidos extraños - In the night, I hear certain strange sounds.

Otro/a, otros/as - another
This can also be used with the article to mean 'the other one'.

Examples:
Me trae otra cerveza, por favor - Can you get me another beer, please?
Este cuadro es feo, prefiero el otro - This painting is ugly, I prefer the other one.

• **Double negatives**
In Spanish the double negative is commonly used. Below are examples of indefinite pronouns/determinants:

algún/a /as/os, ningún/a /as /os - any/none

The above are used to refer to things. They are always used with the noun. If the noun is omitted in case the context is clear, then the forms **alguno** and **ninguno** are used.

- ¿Hay una farmacia aquí? - Is there a chemist shop here?
- No, no hay ninguna - No, there is none.

- ¿Tienes algún libro de español? - Do you have any book in Spanish?
- No, no tengo ninguno - No, I don't have any.

algo, nada - something, nothing
Also refers to things and the negative form is used with **no** as well as without it.

- ¿Tienes algo en el bolso? - Do you have anything in the bag?
- Sí, tengo ... - Yes, I have ...
- No, no tengo nada - No, I don't have anything.

alguien, nadie - someone, nobody
The negative form is used with **no** as well as without it.

- ¿Hay alguien en casa? - Is there anybody at home?
- No, no hay nadie - No, there is nobody.

Nadie viene aquí - Nobody comes here.

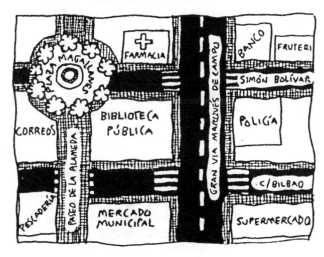

siempre - nunca

These adverbs of time in the negative form are used with **no** as well as without it.

Siempre voy a Madrid durante las vacaciones - I always go to Madrid during the vacations.

No voy nunca a casa de Alfonso - I never go to Alfonso's house.

Nunca vienen a tiempo - They never come on time.

Exercises

1. Fill in the blanks with *un/una/; otro/otra/; ningún/ ninguna/; algo/ nada/; alguien/ nadie*:

a)   ¿Hay .... en casa? No, no hay ......

b)   ¿Tienes ...... bolígrafo? No, no tengo ....

c)   ¿Hay .... para comer? Lo siento, no tengo ......

d)   ¿Tienes ..... carta para mí? No, no hay .....

e)   Esta tienda es muy cara. ¿Vamos a .....?
     Hay ...... cerca de mi casa. Podemos ir allí.

f)   ¿Hay ..... banco en esta calle? No, aquí no hay ......

2. Fill in the blanks with the correct preposition:

1)   ¿.... dónde eres?

2)   Los niños van ..... el colegio en autobús.

3)   Mi abuela sale ...... casa a las siete de la mañana.

4)   ¿Cómo vas .... Madrid? .... tren.

5)   Este autobús pasa .... Bombay.

6)   Mis alumnos quieren pasear ..... el parque.

7)   ¿Tomas el café ...... azúcar?

8)   Trabajo en la oficina .... Gabriel, el primo de Antonio.

9)   La televisión está .... una mesa pequeña.

3. Fill in the blanks with the correct expression: *volver de, salir de, quedar con, empezar a, preocuparse por, ponerse a*.

a)   Esther .... su prima Ana en la puerta del cine.

b)   Mis padres nos traen regalos cuando .... viaje.

c)   En febrero .... estudiar ruso.

d)   Si .... (tú) clase pronto, paso por tu casa.

e)   Carmen .... sus estudios demasiado.

f)   (Yo) .... trabajar después del fútbol.

Unit 4
TELLING THE TIME

Ana pregunta la hora

Ana : ¿Qué hora es?

Pedro: Las 5.

A : ¿Qué haces?

P : Van a venir unos amigos y estoy preparando la cena.

A : ¿A qué hora van a venir?

P : A las nueve. ¿Vas a cenar con nosotros?

A : Lo siento, voy a acostarme temprano, estoy muy cansada.

Ana asks the time

A: What's the time?

P: 5 o'clock.

A: What are you doing?

P: Some friends are coming and I am making the dinner.

A: At what time are they coming?

P: At nine o'clock. Are you going to have dinner with us?

A: I'm sorry, I am going to bed early, I'm very tired.

GRAMMAR

- **Reflexive verbs**

Reflexive verbs are those that refer to the same person as the subject or when the action of the verb is on the same subject, i.e. when the subject and object coincide. It is also used for reciprocal actions. In Spanish the reflexive usage is very common. When the verb is in the infinitive form, the verb is accompanied by the third person pronoun. The Reflexive pronouns are **me, te, se, nos, os, se.**

Examples:

Me levanto a las 6 todas las mañanas - I get up at 6 every morning.

Os laváis las manos. You wash your hands.

Quiero sentarme aquí - I want to sit here.
(When a reflexive verb is used, the possessive pronoun is not used)

Some verbs can be used as reflexive as well as otherwise. In such cases, the meaning changes accordingly.

Examples:
lavar - to wash
lavarse - to wash oneself
levantar - to rise
levantarse - to stand, to get up
poner - to put
ponerse - to put on
quitar - to remove
quitarse - to take off
These are only a few examples that show how the meaning changes when the verb is used reflexively.

Other reflexive verbs:
acostarse - to go to bed
afeitarse - to shave
bañarse - to bathe
despedirse - to say goodbye
despertarse - to wake up
desvestirse - to undress
ducharse - to have a shower
lavarse los dientes/el pelo - to clean the teeth/ to wash one´s hair
maquillarse - to put on make-up
peinarse - to comb
cortarse el pelo - to cut one's hair
cortarse las uñas - to cut one´s nails
hacerse el pelo - to do one´s hair
hacerse una trenza/coleta - to make a plait/ ponytail
pintarse - to put on make-up
quedarse - to remain
sentarse - to sit down
vestirse - to get dressed

- **The verb ir used to express the immediate future**

The expression Ir + a + INFINITIVE expresses the idea of an action which is going to take place in the immediate future.

40

Voy a escribir una carta esta tarde - I am going to write a letter this afternoon.
¿Vas a ver una película de Almodóvar? - Are you going to see an Almodovar film?

The verb **ir in the present tense can be used to denote the future tense** whenever there is an indicator of future time like *la semana/mes/año que viene, mañana, etc.* (next week/ month/ year, tomorrow, etc.) or with the adverb *próximamente* (shortly).

Mañana voy a tu casa - Tomorrow I will go to your house.

* **Expressions with ir**
  ir de *picnic* - **to go for a picnic**
  ir de vacaciones - **to go on a holiday**
  ir de compras - **to go shopping**

ir + en + modes of transport
bicicleta - bicycle, moto - motorcycle, coche - car, camión - truck, autobús - bus, metro - metro(underground), avión - plane, barco - ship, etc.
ir + a + pie, caballo (to go walking, to go on horseback)

* **Adjectives to express repetitive or habitual actions**

Cada + día, mañana, semana, mes, verano, miércoles, etc. - Every day/ morning/ week/ month/ summer/ Wednesday, etc.
Todos los + días, meses, años, miércoles, veranos, etc. - Every day/ month/ year/ Wednesday/ summer, etc.
Todas las + semanas, primaveras, etc - Every week/ spring, etc.

* **Cada + noun - each (noun)**
Cada niño debe leer un cuento - Each child must read a story.
Cada uno de + group - each one (of a group)
Cada uno de nosotros sabe tocar un instrumento - Each one of us knows to play an instrument.

* **La gente** (the people) is singular:
La gente en España come muy tarde - People in Spain eat very late.

For generalisations we use expressions like *todo el mundo, mucha gente, muchas personas* (everybody, many people, many persons)

Todo el mundo quiere ir a España - Everybody wants to go to Spain.

Muchas personas comen tarde - Many people eat late.

- **La mayoría de + countable nouns in plural (Most of ...)**
La mayor parte de + countable/ uncountable nouns (Most of..

La mayoría de los estudiantes no están de huelga - Most of the students aren't on strike.

La mayor parte de la gasolina viene de Rusia. - Most of the petrol comes from Russia.

La mayoría de can also be used with la gente

La mayoría de la gente piensa que Antonio y yo somos hermanos, pero él es mi primo - Most people think that Antonio is my brother, but he is my cousin.

- **único/a/os/as - only**

These are used with the article to single out one element of a group.

Es la única rubia de la familia - She is the only blonde in the family.

- **mismo/a, mismos/as - same**

These also agree in gender and number and are used with articles.

Tengo el mismo libro - I have the same book.

- **Partitive Indefinite Adjectives**

The following adjectives change according to the gender and are used in the singular and plural forms with countable nouns and only in the singular form with uncountable nouns.

Mucho/ mucha - a lot/many
Demasiado/ demasiada - too much/ too many
Poco /poca - very little/ few
Tanto/ tanta - so much/ so many

Examples:

Bebo *mucha* agua en verano - I drink a lot of water in summer.

Tengo *muchos* amigos en España - I have many friends in Spain.

Mi hija toma *demasiada* leche - My daughter drinks too much milk.

Tengo *demasiados* libros en casa - I have too many books at home.

Tiene *tanto* dinero que no sabe cómo gastarlo - He has so much money that he doesn't know how to spend it.

Tengo *tantos* libros que puedo regalarte algunos - I have so many books that I can give you some.

Queda *poca* fruta. Tenemos que comprar - Very little fruit remains. We have to buy some.

Quedan *pocos* huevos en la nevera. There are few eggs remaining in the fridge.

Bastante/s - enough can be used with countable as well as uncountable nouns and agree in number.

Tenemos *bastante* trabajo - We have enough work.

Tienen *bastantes* amigos - They have enough friends.

Mas/menos - more/less can be used with countable as well as uncountable nouns and do not change.

En aquel grupo son *menos* hombres pero tienen *más* fuerza - In that group there are fewer men but they are stronger.

- **Time**

The verb **ser** is used to tell the time and the article **la** or **las** is used with **hora**:

¿Qué hora es? - What is the time?

13.00 (Es) la una (en punto)

15.00 (Son) las tres (en punto)

15.15 (Son) las tres y cuarto

15.20 (Son) las tres y veinte

15.30 (Son) las tres y media

13.35 (Son) las dos menos veinticinco

13.45 (Son) las dos menos cuarto

The preposition **a** is used to ask questions about time:

¿A qué hora comes? - At what time do you eat?
A las tres - At three o'clock.

The preposition **de** is used with **mañana, tarde, noche** when the time is mentioned. Otherwise, **por** is used.

Tengo clase a las siete de la mañana - I have a class at 7 in the morning.
Por la tarde no hay clase - There is no class in the evening.

CARDINAL NUMBERS	
0 cero	26 veintiséis
1 uno (un), una	27 veintisiete
2 dos	28 veintiocho
3 tres	29 veintinueve
4 cuatro	30 treinta
5 cinco	31 treinta y uno (un/una)
6 seis	32 treinta y dos
7 siete	40 cuarenta
8 ocho	50 cincuenta
9 nueve	60 sesenta
10 diez	70 setenta
11 once	80 ochenta
12 doce	90 noventa
13 trece	100 cien/ciento
14 catorce	200 doscientos/as
15 quince	300 trescientos/as
16 dieciséis	400cuatrocientos/as
17 diecisiete	500 quinientos/as
18 dieciocho	600 seiscientos /as
19 diecinueve	700 setecientos/as
20 veinte	800 ochocientos/as
21 veintiuno	900 novecientos/as
22 veintidós	1000 mil
23 veintitrés	2000 dos mil
24 veinticuatro	100.000 cien mil
25 veinticinco	1.000.000 un millón

• There are feminine and masculine forms for the hundreds: doscientos dólares, doscientas liras.

- **Cien** is used alone or with **mil** or **millones** and **ciento** when it is followed by units and tens: ciento quince (115), ciento cuarenta (140).
- With **millón** and **millones** the preposition **de** is used: cinco millones de pesos.
- To express approximate quantities, the indefinite articles **unos, unas** are used: unos diez marcos, unas diez personas.
- To refer to higher or lower quantities with respect to another quantity **más de** or **menos de** in used: más de cuarenta y dos (43, 44, 45, ...), menos de cuarenta y dos (41, 40, 39, ...).

ORDINAL NUMBERS

1º primero
2º segundo
3º tercero
4º cuarto
5º quinto
6º sexto
7º séptimo
8º octavo
9º noveno
10º décimo

- In Spanish the ordinal numbers are used only upto *décimo*, after which the cardinal ones are used.
- Ordinal numbers are like adjectives, that is, they agree in gender and number: vivo en el segundo piso, puerta quinta.
- Primero and tercero lose the last -o when used with a masculine singular noun.

Antonio vive en el tercer piso - Antonio lives on the third floor.
Es el primer viaje que hacemos a Cuba - This is our first trip to Cuba.

Exercises

1. Fill in the blanks with present tense or the periphrasis *ir a + infinitive*:

Todos los lunes (LEVANTARSE, yo) .... a las ocho en punto. (DESAYUNAR, yo) .... café con leche y tostadas casi siempre y luego (IR, yo) .... al gimnasio para hacer un poco de ejercicio. (TRABAJAR, yo) .... en una oficina de correos, casi nunca (COMER, yo) .... en casa porque cerca de la oficina hay un comedor para los trabajadores muy barato; pero la próxima semana (IR + A + COCINAR, yo) .... en casa porque (IR + A + VENIR, ella) .... mi hermana a visitarme. (IR + A + HACER , yo) .... merluza a la vasca. Después de comer, (IR + A+ IR, nosotras) .... de compras y por la noche, al cine.

2. ¿Qué hora es?
12.45
18.20
16.15
20.35
21.30

3. Complete with the correct reflexive pronouns:
a) Antonio siempre .... levanta tarde, pero hoy va a levantar........ a las siete porque tiene que ir al médico.
b) Roberto y Maxi .... quedan en casa esta noche para estudiar.
c) .... despierto a las ocho, pero no .... levanto hasta las ocho y media.
d) Tu hermana siempre .... pinta los labios de rojo, ¿tu también .... los pintas?
e) Vamos a acostar......... (nosotros), ¿vosotros .... quedáis viendo la televisión?

46

Unit 5
WEATHER

Ana y Pedro están hablando en casa.

P: ¡Hola, Ana! Hace días que no nos vemos.

A: Sí...., es que estoy muy ocupada. Esta mañana me he levantado a las seis, he preparado algunas cosas y me he ido a la consulta.

P: ¿Estuviste ayer en la fiesta de Luis?

A: No, me quedé en casa preparando un informe.

P: Yo tampoco fui, me han dicho que fue muy divertida.

A: Por cierto, ¿has comprado pan?, quiero hacerme un bocadillo, esta mañana no he desayunado.

P: Lo siento, he ido a la tienda, pero no han traído pan esta mañana.

Ana le cuenta a su amiga argentina cómo es el tiempo en España.

B: ¿Qué tiempo hace en España en verano, Ana?

A: Bueno, depende. En el norte la temperatura es suave y muy agradable, no hace ni frío ni calor pero llueve a menudo. En el sur hace bastante calor.

B: ¿Y qué tal en invierno?

A: En el centro hace frío, en el sur se está muy bien. En las montañas suele nevar.

B: ¿Qué tal en la costa mediterránea?

A: Está muy bien pero a veces en octubre hay tormentas muy fuertes.

B: ¿Te puedes bañar en invierno?

A: Hace demasiado viento pero yo me he bañado en pleno mes de enero.

Ana and Pedro are talking at home.

P: Hello, Ana! We haven't met for several days.

A: Yes, ... it's just that I'm very busy. This morning I got up at six, I prepared some things and went to the clinic.

P: Were you there in Luis's party yesterday?

A: No, I stayed at home to prepare a report.

P: I too did not go. But I am told that it was very enjoyable.

A: By the way, have you bought bread? I want to make myself a sandwich, I haven't had breakfast this morning.

P: I'm sorry. I went to the bakery, but they didn't have bread today.

Ana speaks to her Argentinean friend about the weather

B: What is the weather like in Spain in summer, Ana?

A: Well, it depends. In the north, the temperature is very moderate and it is pleasant, it is neither hot nor cold but it rains often. In the South it's quite hot.

B: And what about winter?

A: In the centre it is cold but in the south, it is very nice. It usually snows on the mountains.

B: And how about the Mediterranean coast?

A: It is very nice although sometimes in October there are very strong storms.

B: Can you bathe in winter?

A: It is very windy but I have even bathed in the month of January.

USEFUL PHRASES

¿Qué tiempo hace (en Guatemala)?- How's the weather (in Guatemala)?

Está nublado- It's cloudy
Está granizando- It's hailing
Está tronando- It thunders
Está lloviendo - It's raining
Está nevando- It's snowing
Hace buen/mal tiempo- The weather is good/bad
Hace viento/frío/calor/sol- It's windy/cold/hot/sunny
Hay niebla- It's foggy
Hay tormenta- It's stormy

VOCABULARY

(el) rayo	- thunder-bolt	(el) verano	- summer
(el) trueno	- thunder	(el) otoño	- autumn
(el) relámpago	- lightning	(el) invierno	- winter
(la) luna	- moon	(el) norte	- North
(el) sol	- sun	(el) sur	- South
(el) clima	- climate	(el) este	- East
(las) estaciones	- seasons	(el) oeste	- West
(la) primavera	- spring	(el) centro	- Centre

- Expressions with **tener**:

tener calor - to feel hot
tener frío - to feel cold
tener ganas de - to desire
tener hambre - to be hungry
tener prisa - to be in a hurry
tener razón - to be right
tener sed - to be thirsty
tener sueño - to be sleepy

GRAMMAR

- **Describing the weather**

The verb **hacer** is used to describe the weather. It is only used in the third person singular form:
hace fresco, hace sol, hace buen/mal tiempo, etc.

Examples:
Hace calor - It is hot.
Hace viento - It is windy.
Hace mucho frío en los meses de diciembre y enero - It is very cold in the months of December and January.

The verb **ser** is used with temperature:
Las temperaturas son muy altas en el mes de mayo - The temperatures are very high in the month of May.

There are some **impersonal verbs** like **nevar, llover, granizar,** which are also used only in the third person singular form:
Llueve mucho - It is raining a lot / It rains a lot.
En las montañas nieva bastante - In the mountains it snows quite a lot.

• Days of the week:

lunes	- Monday	(el) fin de semana	- week end
martes	- Tuesday	(el) día festivo	- holiday
miércoles	- Wednesday	(las) vacaciones	- vacations
jueves	- Thursday	(la) jornada	- shift
viernes	- Friday	media jornada	- half-day
sábado	- Saturday	jornada intensiva	- continuous shift
domingo	- Sunday	trabajo a tiempo parcial	- part-time job
(el) día laborable	- working day		

Note: All the days of the week are masculine and are used with the masculine singular and plural articles. The plural forms are the same except **sábados** and **domingos**. The plurals are used for generalising or for repetitive actions.

Examples:
Los lunes tengo clase de inglés -I have English classes on Mondays.

• Date and months

1, 2, 3.... 30, 31 + DE + enero, febrero, marzo, abril, mayo, junio, julio, agosto, septiembre, octubre, noviembre, diciembre + DE + 1999.

Example:
El 3 de septiembre de 1976.
The article is used with the date except with **hoy (today)**
Hoy es 12 de abril - Today is the 12th of April.
Mi cumpleaños es el 22 de diciembre - My birthday is on 22nd December.

• Present Perfect

The Present Perfect tense is used to express a complete action when the time frame of the action is not over. Therefore, it has some relation to the present.

It is formed with the present tense of the auxillary verb **haber** and the **past participle**.

he
has
he   + habl-**ado**
hemos   com-**ido**
habéis   viv-**ido**
han

The participles are formed by adding -**ado** to verbs ending in -*ar* and -**ido** to verbs ending in -*er* and -*ir*.

Some irregular participles:

escribir	- escrito	poner	- puesto
decir	- dicho	leer	- leído
hacer	- hecho	oír	- oído
romper	- roto	volver	- vuelto
abrir	- abierto	morir	- muerto
ver	- visto		

The **Present Perfect Tense** is used with the following time sequences:
Hoy - Today
Este/a mañana (tarde, semana, mes, año) - This morning (afternoon, week, month, year)
Alguna vez - Ever
Nunca - Never

Examples:
Esta mañana hemos visto una película interesante - This morning we have seen an interesting film.
Nunca he comido paella - I have never eaten paella.
¿Has estado alguna vez en India? - Have you ever been to India?

Indicators of time:

siempre	- always	a veces	- sometimes
casi siempre	- almost always	casi nunca	- almost never
normalmente	- normally	nunca	- never

• **ya - already**

todavía/ aún - still
todavía no/ aún no - yet
The above are also used with the Perfect Tense.

Examples:

¿Ya ha venido Ana? - Has Ana already come?
¿Todavía estás aquí? - Are you still here?
¿Aún no has comido? - Haven't you eaten still?

Ya no is used to express an interruption in the action.
¿Qué tal en la universidad?
Bien, pero ya no trabajo allí.
How are things at the University?
Fine, but I am no longer working there.

Ya is also used in the sense of **inmediatamente, sin dejar pasar más el tiempo** (immediately, right away):
- Iré a las siete.
- Vete ya.
- I will go at 7 o'clock.
- Go right away.

- **Past Indefinite**

The Past Indefinite Tense is used to express a complete action in a definite and concrete time frame in the past. It is conjugated as follows:

hablar	comer	vivir
habl-**é**	com-**í**	viv-**í**
habl-**aste**	com-**iste**	viv-**iste**
habl-**ó**	com-**ió**	viv-**ió**
habl-**amos**	com-**imos**	viv-**imos**
habl-**asteis**	com-**isteis**	viv-**isteis**
habl-**aron**	com-**ieron**	viv-**ieron**

(See Appendix 2 for conjugation of irregular verbs).

It is used with the following time sequences:

Ayer	- yesterday	Anoche	- last night
Anteayer	- day before yesterday	Anteanoche	- Night before last

El/la semana (mes, año, verano...) pasado/a - Last week, (month, year, summer...)
Hace (dos) días (meses, años) - (Two) days (months, years) ago.

Examples:

Ayer hablé con Luis - Yesterday I spoke to Luis.

El verano pasado me visitaron mis amigos - My friends visited me last summer.

Hace dos días estuve en Madrid - I was in Madrid two days ago.

Exercises

1. Use the verbs given in brackets in the Present Perfect or Past Indefinite Tenses:

a) ¿Qué (HACER, tú) .... esta tarde? Te (LLAMAR, yo) .... por teléfono dos veces.

b) ¿(ESTAR, tú) .... en París alguna vez?

Sí, (ESTAR, yo) .... el año pasado, en abril.

c) El sábado por la mañana (IR, yo) .... a la playa con mi hermana y por la tarde (ESTAR, yo) .... en casa. ¿Y tú? ¿Qué (HACER) .... este fin de semana?

d) La calle está mojada ¿(LLOVER) .... esta noche?

e) El verano pasado (IR, nosotros) .... a Barcelona. ¿(IR, vosotros) .... alguna vez?.

2. Imagine that last month you did some extraordinary things, write them down so as not to forget:

Example:

el lunes pasado, ir a la radio, participar en un concurso de canciones, ganar un millón de pesetas

El lunes pasado fui a la radio, participé en un concurso de televisión y gané un millón de pesetas.

a) el miércoles pasado, ir a una reunión importante, estropearse el coche, llegar dos horas tarde

b) el sábado pasado, ir de excursión con unos amigos, empezar a llover mucho, quedarse a dormir en un hotel de la carretera

c) la semana pasada, no ir a trabajar, quedarse en casa para descansar, venir un amigo de India de visita, estar hablando todo el día, no descansar nada.

3. Choose the correct elements from three columns and make sentences:

El otro día	Marcos	estuvimos	cenando en casa de unos amigos
El verano pasado	mi marido y yo	hemos ido	los regalos de navidad
El martes	Ø	fue	los deberes muy bien
Hace dos días		me quedé	al médico
Esta semana		hicimos	a Roma de vacaciones
Esta mañana		he comprado	en casa sola
Ya		ha hecho	un pastel riquísimo

Unit 6
EATING OUT

Ana y Pedro van a un restaurante.

Camarero- ¿Qué desean tomar?

Ana- ¿Qué nos sugiere?

C: En la carta está el menú del día, que es riquísimo.

A: A ver... (mirando la carta), sí, me gusta. De primero, voy a tomar gazpacho andaluz y de segundo, merluza a la vasca.

C: ¿Y el señor qué desea?

P: Yo no tengo mucha hambre, tráigame una ensalada y algo de picar.

C: ¿Le traigo unas tapas entonces?

A: Sí, un poco de jamón y de queso.

C: ¿Para beber?

P: Dos cañas.

C: ¿Qué quieren de postre?

A: Para mí, tarta de chocolate.

P: Yo no quiero nada.

C: ¿Van a tomar café?

A: Sí, por favor. ¿Tú quieres, Pedro?

P: Sí, un cortado.

A: Nos trae la cuenta también, por favor.

Pedro le pide a Ana la receta del gazpacho.

P: Oye Ana, ¿cómo se hace el gazpacho?

A: Pues, muy fácil: lava los tomates, un kilo más o menos, y dos o tres pimientos, luego corta cebolla en trozos grandes y dos o tres ajos. Mételo todo en la batidora y echa sal y pimienta.

P: ¿Las verduras crudas?

A: Sí, claro.

P: ¿Los tomates no se pelan?

A: No hace falta, pero si quieres, pélalos.

P: Gracias, voy a probar.

Ana and Pedro go to a restaurant.

Waiter: What would you like to have, please?

A: What do you recommend?

W: In the menu card, you can see the dish of the day. It is very tasty.

A: Let's have a look... (looking at the menu), yes, I like it. For the first course, I'll have Andalucian Gazpacho, for the second I'll have hake prepared in Basque style.

W: And the gentleman, what would he like?

P: I'm not too hungry, bring me a salad and something to munch.

W: Shall I bring some snacks?

P: Yes, a bit of ham and cheese.

W: And drinks?

P: Two beers.

.....

W: What would you like for dessert?

A: A chocolate pastry for me.

P: I don't want anything.

W: Will you have coffee?

A: Yes, please. Do you want coffee, Pedro?

P: Yes, coffee with milk.

A: Please bring the bill as well.

Pedro asks Ana how to make gazpacho.

P: Listen Ana, how do you make gazpacho?.

A: Well, it's very easy; you wash the tomatoes, a kilo or so, two or three capsicums and cut onions in big pieces and two or three cloves of garlic. Put it all in the mixer and add salt and pepper.

P: The vegetables are to be put in raw?

A: Yes, of course.

P: Do you peel the tomatoes?

A: Well, it is not necessary, but if you want, you can peel them.

P: Thank you, I am going to try it out.

USEFUL PHRASES

Aquí tiene la carta - Here is the menu.

¿Qué desean tomar?- What would you like to order?

¿Qué nos sugiere?- What do you suggest?

¿Quieren algunas tapas?- Would you like to have some snacks?

¿Cuál es el menú del día? - What's on the menu today?

Tráigame (una tarta de chocolate), por favor? - Bring me (a chocolate pastry), please?

(No) tengo hambre - I am (not) hungry.

Nos trae la cuenta, por favor - Please bring us the bill.

¿Puedo pagar con tarjeta de crédito? - Can I pay with a credit card?

¿Cuánto tardarán? - How long will it take?

Es para llevar - It is to take away.

La comida está fría - The food is cold.

La comida está muy salada - The food is very salty.

Quisiera hablar con el dueño - I'd like to talk to the manager.

¿Cómo se hace (el gazpacho)?- How does one make (gazpacho)?

(la) carta	- menu	(el) segundo plato	- second course
camarero	- waiter		
(la) cuenta	- bill	(el) postre	- dessert
(la) propina	- tip	(la) mesa reservada	- booked table
(el) primer plato	- first course		

Places to eat

(el) restaurante	- restaurant	(el) bar	- bar
(la) cafetería	- café	(la) pizzería	- a pizza shop

VOCABULARY

Some Spanish Dishes

Tortilla española	-	Spanish omelette (with potatoes)
Gazpacho andaluz	-	a cold soup made with tomatoes
Merluza a la vasca	-	hake prepared in Basque style
Paella valenciana	-	a rice dish with meat, vegetables or fish
Fabada asturiana	-	kidney beans with meat
Cocido	-	vegetable or meat stew
Callos	-	tripe

Some Latin American Dishes

Cebiche	-	a Peruvian dish (fish with lemon)
Ajiaco	-	Cuban, Colombian dish (vegetable, chicken, pepper and capers)

Enchiladas - Mexican dish (puré of flour, meat and chilli)
Tacos   - Mexican dish (rolled tortilla)
Asado   - Argentinean dish (roast beef, barbacued beef)

Food

(el)PESCADO	- fish

(el) MARISCO	- sea food
(las) gambas	- prawns
(la) langosta	- lobster

(la) CARNE	- meat
(el) cordero	- lamb, mutton
(la) ternera	- beef
(el) pollo	- chicken
(el) cerdo	- pork
(el) jamón	- ham
(la) salchicha	- sausage
(el) salchichón	- salami
(el) chorizo	- hard pork sausage

(la) FRUTA	- fruit
(la) manzana	- apple
(la) naranja	- orange
(la) pera	- pear
(la) uva	- grape
(el) plátano	- banana
(el) melocotón	- peach
(el) melón	- melon
(la) sandía	- watermelon

(la) fresa	- strawberry
(la) cereza	- cherry
(la) piña	- pineapple

(la) VERDURA	- vegetable
(las) espinacas	- spinach
(las) judías verdes	- French beans
(la) lechuga	- lettuce
(el) tomate	- tomato
(la) patata	- potato
(la) cebolla	- onion
(el) ajo	- garlic
(el) pimiento	- capsicum
(los) guisantes	- peas
(los) espárragos	- asparagus
(los) champiñones	- mushrooms
(la) calabaza	- pumpkin
(la) col	- cabbage
(la) coliflor	- cauliflower
(la) berenjena	- brinjal
(la) zanahoria	- carrot

(los)LEGUMBRES	- pulses
(los) garbanzos	- chick peas
(las) lentejas	- lentils
(las) alubias	- kidney beans

Cooking

(la) sal	- salt
(la) pimienta	- pepper
(la) guindilla/ pimienta cayena	- chilli
(el) vinagre	- vinegar
(el) azúcar	- sugar

(la) leche	- milk
(la) harina	- flour
(el) huevo	- egg
(la) mantequilla	- butter
(el) aceite	- oil
(el) pastel, (la) tarta	- cake

(la) ensalada	- salad	(la) tostada	- toast
(las) aceitunas	- olives	(el) puré	- puré
(el) queso	- cheese	(el) bocadillo	- sandwich
(la) nata	- cream	(el) hielo	- ice
(el) yogur	- yogurt	(el) helado	- ice-cream
(la) mermelada	- jam	(la) sopa	- soup
(el) caldo	- broth, clear soup	(la) miel	- honey
		(el) zumo	- fruit juice

Kitchen Utensils And Electrodomestics

(el) plato	- plate	(el) abrelatas	- tin opener
(el) vaso	- glass	(los) cubiertos	- cutlery
(el) cuchillo	- knife	(la) servilleta	- napkin
(el) tenedor	- fork	(el) mantel	- tablecloth
(la) cuchara	- spoon	(el) cenicero	- ashtray
(el) colador	- strainer	(la) cocina	- stove
(la) sartén	- frying pan	(el) horno	- oven
(la) olla	- vessel	(la) nevera	- refrigerator
(la) cacerola/ (la) cazuela	- casserole	(el) congelador	- freezer
(la) fiambrera	- lunchbox	(el) lavaplatos/ (el) lavavajillas	- dishwasher
(el) bote	- glass bottle	(la) batidora	- mixer
(la) botella	- bottle	(la) picadora	- chopper
(el) cuenco	- bowl	(la) lavadora	- washing machine
(la) fuente	- dish		
(la) jarra	- jug	(el) grifo	- tap
(la) taza	- cup	(el) fregadero	- sink
(el) abridor de botellas	- bottle opener		

Drinks

(el) agua	- water	(la) cerveza (caña)	- beer
- mineral	- mineral water		
(el) vino	- wine	(el) café	- coffee
- blanco	- white	- solo	- black coffee
- rosado	- rose	- cortado	- coffee with a little milk
- tinto	- red		
(el) refresco	- cold drink	- con leche	- coffee with milk
(la) sangría	- a fruit punch made with vine and fruits	(la) infusión	- infusion
		(el) té	- tea

59

Meals

desayunar	- to breakfast	(el) desayuno	- breakfast
almorzar	- to have lunch	(el) almuerzo	- midday meal
comer	- to eat	(la) comida	- lunch
merendar	- to have tea	(la) merienda	- tea
cenar	- to dine	(la) cena	- dinner

Some verbs about cooking

picar (algo)	- to munch/to mince	echar/meter/ poner	- to put in
hervir	- to boil		
asar	- to roast	cocinar	- to cook
freir	- to fry	cortar	- to cut
tostar	- to toast	probar	- to taste
lavar	- to clean	calentar	- to heat
pelar	- to peel	enfriar	- to cool

Adjectives to describe food

They can be used with the verbs *ser* or *estar*. *Ser* is used with inherent characteristics and *estar* is used to describe the taste of a particular food.

picante	- spicy	soso	- tasteless/ saltless
amargo	- bitter	salado	- salty
dulce	- sweet	caliente	- hot
agrio	- sour	templado	- warm
rico, bueno	- tasty	crudo	- raw
malo	- bad	cocido	- cooked
		fresco	- fresh

Examples:

La tortilla está salada. - The omlette is salty.

La guindilla es muy picante - The chilli is very spicy.

Quantities

una lata de atún	-	a tin of tuna
un kilo de azúcar	-	a kilo of sugar
medio kilo de café	-	half a kilo of coffee
un cuarto de harina	-	a quarter of flour
una botella de aceite	-	a bottle of oil
una docena de huevos	-	a dozen eggs
un litro de leche	-	a litre of milk
una rebanada de pan	-	a slice of bread

GRAMMAR

- **The Imperative/ Command**

The Imperative is used to give orders, to request or to advise someone to do something. It has different forms for **tú, vosotros, usted and ustedes** for the affirmative as well as the negative. In the box below, we give the conjugation pattern (affirmative and negative) of regular verbs:

Affirmative Forms		
	- ar	-er/-ir
Tú	pas-**a**	com-**e**
Usted	pas-**e**	com-**a**
Vosotros	pas-**ad**	com-**ed**
Ustedes	pas-**en**	com-**an**
Negative forms		
Tú	No pas-**es**	No com-**as**
Usted	No pas-**e**	No com-**a**
Vosotros	No pas-**éis**	No com-**áis**
Ustedes	No pas-**en**	No com-**an**

(See Appendix 2 for irregular forms).

Examples:
Abre la ventana, por favor. - Open the window, please.
Haced los deberes para mañana - Do the homework for tomorrow.
No comas chocolate - Don't eat chocolate.

All irregular verbs in the present tense are also irregular in the imperative. The irregular imperative forms of the second person singular (**tú**) are given in the appendix.

Examples:
Sal de aquí. - Go away from here.
Ven aqui - Come here.

The other three forms (**vosotros, usted, ustedes**) as well all the negative forms are derived from the *1st person singular form of the Present Indicative*. The endings of -*ar* ending verbs changes to -**e** and the ending of -*er/ -ir* verbs changes to -**a**.

Examples:
Salir - salgo - salg-**a**
tener - tengo - teng-**a**
cerrar - cierro - cierr-**e**

In the case of reflexive verbs, the pronoun comes after the verb in an affirmative sentence and before the verb in a negative sentence.

Examples:
Lávate las manos antes de comer - Wash your hands before eating.
No se levante tan temprano - Don't get up so early.

For use of object pronouns with the imperatives, please see the next part of this unit.

- **Object Pronouns**

These are of two kinds - Direct and Indirect Object Pronouns.

In a sentence like *Carmen regala flores a su madre* (Carmen gifts flowers to her mother) there are two objects: *flores* and *a su madre*. The first is a direct object and the second an indirect object.

The **direct object pronouns** are as follows:

	Singular	Plural
First person	me	nos
Second person	te	os
Third person	lo, la	los, las

The **indirect object pronouns** are as follows:

	Singular	Plural
First person	me	nos
Second person	te	os
Third person	le	les

Position of object pronouns:

The indirect object pronoun is always put before the direct object pronoun in a sentence.

When **le, les** (the third person indirect object pronouns) come before **lo, la, los, las** (the third person direct object pronouns), they are written as **se**.

The position of the object pronouns also varies according to the verb tenses as given below.

• **With the present tense**

The object pronouns are placed before the conjugated verb and can be placed before or after if the verb is in the infinitive.

Examples:

-¿Hago la comida?(Direct Object)

- Sí, puedes hacer**la**

Nosotros escribimos cartas (Direct Object) a nuestros padres (Indirect Object).

Nosotros **se las** escribimos.

Quiero dar este libro (Direct Object) a Juan (Indirect Object).

Quiero dár**selo**.

- **With the Imperative**

In the imperative, the object pronouns are placed after the verb in the case of the affirmative forms (written as one word) and before the verb in the case of the negative forms:

Examples:
Cierra la ventana - Ciérra**la**
Coge el bolígrafo - Cóge**los**
Traiga el café a mí - Tráe**melo**
Dame esos vasos - Dá**melos**

No abras esta puerta - No **la** abras.
No me traigan estos libros - No **me los** traigan

- **With the Present Perfect and the Present Continuous Tenses**

In the Present Perfect Tense the object pronouns are placed before the verb and in the Present Continuous Tense they are placed after the gerund (written as one word).

Examples:
¿Te has comido la manzana? ¿Te **la** has comido?
Estoy cerrando la ventana. Estoy cerrándo**la**.

Exercises

1. Use imperatives to complete the following sentences:
   a) (Coger, tú) ..... la primera calle a la derecha y después (seguir, tú)....... todo recto hasta el final de la calle.
   b) (Traer (a mí), usted) ...... el libro, por favor.
      No (hacer, usted) ..... ruido, por favor.
      (Sentarse, usted) ..... en este sillón.
   c) (Coger, vosotros) .... el autobús 44 y (bajar, vosotros) ..... en la segunda parada.
   d) (Hacer, tú) ..... los deberes y (venir, tú) ..... a mi casa después.
   e) No (comer, vosotros) ..... estas frutas.
      (Cerrar, vosotros) ..... esta puerta y no (hablar, vosotros).....

2. Substitute the words in brackets with the correct object pronouns and rewrite the sentence:
   a) María ha regalado (unas flores) (a Juan).
   b) Da (los libros) (a Luis).
   c) Coge (la sal) y echa (sal) a la comida.
   d) (Tú) prueba (el vestido).
   e) Traiga (un libro) (para mí)
   f) He comprado (las naranjas) en el mercado.

3. Complete with *se* or *le*:
   a) A Juan ..... duele la cabeza mucho, tiene que descansar.
   b) ¿A qué hora .... levanta tu marido?
   c) ¿......... puede comer en esta sala?
   d) A Jorge no .... gusta quedar...... en Madrid en agosto.
   e) A Gema .... molesta tu actitud, tienes que cambiar.
   f) Dá.....lo enseguida porque lo necesita.
   g) Regála..... un disco por su cumpleaños.

4. Translate the following sentences into Spanish:
   a) Give it to me soon because I need it. (the knife – el cuchillo)
   b) I will have to keep it to have a look at it at home (the notebook - la libreta)
   c) You have eaten all of them (the apples – las manzanas)
   d) Why don't you read them in class? (the books – los libros)
   e) They wear them every Sunday (the skirts – las faldas)

Unit 7
TRAVELLING

Ana espera en el aeropuerto a una amiga.

A: ¿A qué hora llega el vuelo B487?

B: A las 12.05, pero lleva un retraso de 20 minutos.

A: ¿Podría cancelar un vuelo para Argentina que tenía reservado?

B: ¿Con qué compañía?

A: Iberia. El número de vuelo no lo sé, pero sale el 20 de diciembre a las ocho de la noche y hace escala en Londres.

B: Sí, ya lo tiene cancelado. ¿Quiere hacer otra reserva?

A: De momento no, gracias.

Pedro está en la estación de trenes.

Pedro- ¿A qué hora sale el tren para Barcelona?

Sr. Fernández- A las 11.35 y llega a Barcelona a las 7 de la tarde.

P: ¿Quedan plazas?

F: Sí, en primera.

P: ¿Y cuánto cuesta?

F: 7.500 ida y vuelta.

P: ¿Hay descuento para estudiantes?

F: En primera, no. Lo siento.

P: Está bien. Deme tres billetes.

F: ¿Fumador o no fumador?

P: No fumador.

Pedro, Ana y Juan están en el tren.

P: ¿Qué haremos al llegar?

A: Buscaremos un sitio para dormir y luego iremos a cenar ¿no?

J: Mañana veremos el Museo Picasso ¿vale?

P: Y por la tarde, visitaremos la Sagrada Familia, el Parc Güell, etc.

A: El domingo comeremos en casa de tus amigos ¿verdad?

P: Sí, está claro.

Ana is in the airport waiting for a friend

A: At what time does the flight B487 reach?

B: At 12.05, but it is late by 20 minutes.

A: Could I cancel a reserved ticket for Argentina?

B: With which airline?

A: Iberia. I don't know the flight number but it is for the 20 of December at 8 p.m via London.

B: Yes, it is already cancelled. Do you wish to make another reservation?

A: Not for the moment, thank you.

Pedro is in the railway station.

Pedro: At what time is the train for Barcelona?

Sr. Fernández: At 11.35 and it reaches Barcelona at 7 p.m.

P: Are there any seats left?

F: Yes, in first class.

P: How much is it?

P: 7,500 back and forth.

P: Is there a discount for students?

F: Not in the first class, I'm sorry.

P: OK. Give me three tickets.

F: Smoking or non-smoking.

P: Non smoking.

Pedro, Ana and Juan are on the train.

P: What will we do on reaching Barcelona?

A: We will look for a place to sleep and then, we'll go and eat something.

J: Tomorrow we'll go to the Picasso Museum, isn't it?

P: And in the evening, we'll visit the Sagrada Familia, Güell Park, etc.

A: We'll eat in your friend's house on Sunday, right?

P: Yes, of course.

USEFUL PHRASES
General information

Estoy aquí de vacaciones/ de negocios - I'm here on vacation/ business.

Quiero ir a (Madrid) - I want to go to (Madrid).

Estoy con mi familia/ mi amigo/ un grupo - I'm with my family/ a friend/ a group.

General enquiries at the airport/ rail station

¿Han retrasado el tren/ vuelo? - Is the train/ flight going to be delayed?

¿El tren/ avión (sale) llega con retraso? - Is the flight (going to be) delayed?

¿Cuánto tardará en llegar? - How long will it take to reach?

¿Hay un autobús para ir al Hotel Eslava? - Is there a bus that will take me to Hotel Eslava?

¿Cómo puedo llegar a ….? - How do I reach …?

¿Dónde puedo coger un taxi? - Where can I get a taxi?

¿Dónde está(n) ….? - Where is/ are ….?

….. la información - information

….. los andenes - the platforms

….. la cafetería - the snack-bar

….. el banco - the bank

….. la consigna - the left luggage

….. la sala de espera - the waiting room

….. los servicios - the toilets

Luggage problems

¿Me puede ayudar con el equipaje? - Can you help me with the luggage?

He perdido el bolso - I've lost my bag.

Me han robado la maleta - My suitcase has been stolen.

No ha llegado mi equipaje - My luggage has not arrived.

Getting information at the airport/ railway station/ bus station:

¿A qué hora hay trenes /vuelos, etc. para (Sevilla)?- At what time is there a train/flight for (Sevilla)?

68

¿A qué hora es el primer/ el siguiente/ el último (vuelo)? - At what time is the first/ next/ last (flight)?

¿Se puede ir en autobús/ coche/ avión/ tren/ etc.? - Can one go by bus car/ plane/ train/ etc.?

¿A qué hora llega el autobús de (Santander)? - At what time does the bus from (Santander) reach?

¿A qué hora sale el autobús para Alicante? - At what time does the bus for Alicante leave?

¿Cuánto tarda en llegar? - How long does it take to reach there?

¿Este/a autobús/ carretera/ tren/ autopista va a (Córdoba)? - Does this bus/ road/ train/ highway go to (Córdoba)?

¿Este/a autobús/carretera/ tren/ autopista/ pasa por (Chimbote)? - Does this bus/road /train/ highway go through (Chimbote)?

¿Este autobús/tren para en (Santiago)? - This bus/train stops at (Santiago)?

¿Hay vuelo a (Roma) hoy?- Is there a flight for (Rome) today?

Getting a ticket

¿Podría darme un billete sencillo para (Barcelona)? - Can you give me a one-way ticket for (Barcelona)?

Quisiera un billete de ida y vuelta para (Córdoba) - I'd like a return ticket for (Córdoba).

¿Cuánto es? - How much is it?

¿Ventana o pasillo?- Window or passage?

¿Fumador o no fumador?- Smoking or Non-smoking?

¿Qué número de asiento tiene?- What is your seat number?

¿Está libre este asiento? - Is this seat vacant?

Sightseeing

¿Dónde está la Oficina de Turismo? - Where is the Tourist Office?

¿Tienen información sobre (el museo)? - Do you have information on (the museum)?

¿Hay viajes para (Toledo)? - Are there any trips to (Toledo)?

¿Cuánto cuesta esta excursión? - How much does this excursion cost?

¿A qué hora salen? - At what time do they leave?

¿A qué hora volvemos? - At what time do we get back?

¿Hay un guía que hable inglés? - Is there a guide who speaks English?

¿Se puede hacer fotos aquí? - Can one take photographs here?
¿Tienen una guía en inglés? - Do you have a guidebook in
English?
¿Está abierto el museo hoy? - Is the museum open today?
¿A qué hora abren? - What time do they open?

See Unit 3 for getting around in the city

VOCABULARY

Getting around

(la) agencia de viajes	- travel agency	(el) billete	- ticket
(la) guía	- guide book	(el) billete de ida y vuelta	- to and fro ticket
(el) destino	- destination	(el) billete sencillo	- single ticket
procedente de	- from		
(la) salida	- departure	(el) suplemento	- surcharge
(la) llegada	- arrival	(el) descuento	- discount
(la) fecha	- date	(la) consigna	- left-luggage office
viajero/a	- traveller	confirmar	- to confirm
turista	- tourist	reservar	- to reserve
conductor	- driver	cancelar	- to cancel

Travelling by Air

(el) avión	-	plane
(el) aeropuerto	-	airport
(la) terminal	-	terminal
(la) compañía aérea	-	airlines
(el) vuelo	-	flight
azafato/a	-	steward, air-hostess
piloto	-	pilot
pasajero/a	-	passenger
(la) aduana	-	customs
(el) control de pasaportes	-	passport control
(la) facturación de equipajes	-	lugagge registration (to check-in)
exceso de equipaje	-	excess baggage
exceso de peso	-	excess weight
(el) equipaje de mano	-	hand baggage
(la) puerta de embarque	-	boarding gate

70

(la) tarjeta de embarque	-	boarding card
embarcar	-	to board
hacer escala	-	to stop over/ to get a connecting flight

Travelling by bus

(la) estación de autobuses	-	bus terminal
(la) parada de autobuses	-	bus stop
(la) dársena	-	dock

Travelling by train

(la) estación de tren	- railway station	(el) coche -cama	- sleeping wagon
(la) vía	- track	(la) litera	- berth, bunk
(el) andén	- platform	revisor	- ticket checker

Travelling by ship

(el) barco	- ship	(la) cabina	- cabin
(el) puerto	- port	(la) cubierta	- deck
(el) muelle	- wharf/docks		

Travelling by car

(el) coche	- car	(el) embrague	- clutch
(el) permiso de conducir	- driving license	(el) acelerador	- accelerator
		(el) freno	- brake
(el) plano	- map	(la) guantera	- glove compartment
(la) acera	- pavement		
(el) arcén	- border	(el) intermitente	- blinker
(la) calzada	- roadway	(el) limpia -parabrisas	- windscreen wiper
(la) carretera	- road		
(el) carril	- track, lane	(el) neumático	- tyre
(el) autopista	- motorway	(la) rueda	- wheel
(el) peaje	- toll	(el) gasóleo	- petrol oil
(el) aparcamiento	- parking	(la) gasolina	- petrol
(el) garaje	- garage	(la) gasolinera	- petrol station
(la) grúa	- crane	(el) límite de velocidad	- speed limit
(la) multa	- fine		
(el) cinturón de seguridad	- safety belt	ceder el paso	- to give way
		adelantar	- to overtake

GRAMMAR

Future Tense

The future tense is conjugated in the following manner:

hablar	comer	vivir
hablar-**é**	comer-**é**	vivir-**é**
hablar-**ás**	comer-**ás**	vivir-**ás**
hablar- **á**	comer-**á**	vivir-**á**
hablar-**emos**	comer-**emos**	vivir-**emos**
hablar-**éis**	comer-**éis**	vivir-**éis**
hablar-**án**	comer-**án**	vivir-**án**

The irregular verbs undergo a transformation in the stem but the endings remain the same.

See Appendix 2 for irregular verb conjugations

The future tense is used to describe actions in the future tense. It is used with the following time sequences:

mañana - tomorrow
pasado mañana - day after tomorrow
el próximo mes/ verano/ año - next month/ summer/ year
la semana que viene - the coming week

Examples:
El año que viene iré a España - Next year I will go to Spain.
Mañana los alumnos vendrán a clase - Tomorrow the students will come to class.

72

Exercises

1. Fill in the blanks with the correct form of the future tense:
a) Las próximas vacaciones (VIAJAR, nosotros) .... a
    Bombay.
b) Julio (VENIR) .... a visitarme esta tarde.
c) El sábado que viene (ESTUDIAR, vosotros) ....
    mucho.
d) El verano que viene (CUMPLIR, ella) .... nueve años.
e) Las próximas elecciones (GANAR, ellos) .... los
    socialistas.
f) ¿(INVITAR, tú) .... a tus amigos a la fiesta?

2. Fill in the blanks with the correct prepositions:
a) El tren sale .... Valencia .... las 12.35 y llega
    .... Barcelona .... las 16.05. Pasa .... Castellón
    y Tarragona pero no para .... ninguna estación.
b) Iré .... Lisboa el miércoles .... la tarde y no volveré
    .... Portugal hasta el mes siguiente.
c) Cuando salía .... tu casa me encontré .... tu
    hermana Carmen, entré .... tu casa de nuevo y
    esperamos .... Miguel durante una hora .... ir al
    cine.
d) Pregunta .... Juan si mi amiga Esther viene ....
    autobús o .... tren y .... qué hora llega.

3. Choose the condition from column A and the consequence
    from column B and make sentences as in the example:
    Si no llueve, iré a tu casa

A	B
ganar quinientas mil pesetas (yo)	comprar un coche nuevo (mi marido y yo)
sacar buenas notas (mi hermana)	invitar a una cena a un buen restaurante (yo)
aprobar el carnet de conducir (Carmen)	estar muy contenta (su familia)
comprar un pastel de chocolate (yo)	invitar a mis vecinos (yo)

73

Unit 8
ACCOMMODATION

Ana, Pedro y Juan están en Ibiza. Van a un hotel.

Recepcionista- Buenos días.

A: Hola, buenos días ¿Tienen habitaciones libres?

R: Depende, ¿qué tipo de habitación quieren?

A: Pues, una triple con baño.

P: Y si puede ser, exterior.

R: Tenemos una, pero es interior. Si quieren exterior tendrán que ser dos habitaciones, una doble y una sencilla.

J: ¿Y cuánto cuestan?

R: La triple 6.500 pesetas, la doble 4.500 y la sencilla 2.800.

A: ¿Incluye desayuno?

R: No. Pero el hotel dispone de cafetería y servicio de habitaciones.

P: ¿Podemos ver la habitación?

R: Sí, claro. Es la 209, en el segundo piso, a la derecha del ascensor. El botones les acompaña.

...

R: Entonces, ¿se quedan con la triple?

P: Sí.

R: ¿Me dejan su pasaporte o documento nacional de identidad?

A: Sí, tome. El hotel tiene piscina, ¿verdad?

R: Sí, está saliendo por esa puerta a la derecha. ¿Cuántas noches van a quedarse?

P: De momento, tres.

Ana, Pedro and Juan are in Ibiza. They go to a hotel.

Receptionist: Good morning

A: Hello, good morning. Do you have vacant rooms?

R: It depends. What kind of room do you want?

A: Well, a triple room with a bath.

P: And if possible, a room overlooking the exterior.

74

R: We have one, but it is interior. If you want exterior, then it will have to be two rooms, a double and a single.
J: And how much would they cost?
R: The triple is for 6,500 pesetas, the double costs 4,500 and the single, 2,800.
A: Does it include breakfast?
R: No, but the hotel has a café and room service.
P: Can we see the room?
R: Yes, of course. It is Room 209, on the second floor, to the right of the lifts. The bell boy will accompany you.
...
R: So you want the triple room?
P: Yes.
R: Can you give me your passport or identity card?
A: Yes, here it is. The hotel has a swimming pool, right?
R: Yes, it's on the right as you go out of this door. How many nights are you going to stay?
P: Three, for the moment.

USEFUL PHRASES

Getting Accommodation

¿Hay habitaciones libres? - Are there rooms available?
Lo siento, está lleno - I'm sorry, we're full.
¿Hay otro hotel por aquí cerca? - Is there any other hotel nearby?
¿Cuál es el precio por día?- What is the rent per day?
¿Tienen habitaciones más baratas?- Do you have cheaper rooms?
¿Puedo ver la habitación?- Can I see the room?
¿Tiene más habitaciones?- Do you have more rooms?

¿Tiene baño?- Does it have an attached bathroom?
¿Tiene agua caliente?- Does it have hot water?
¿Tiene calefacción? - Does it have heating?
¿Tiene aire acondicionado? Does it have air-conditioning?

Quisiera una habitación con baño - I'd like a room with a bath.

Rellene este formulario, por favor - Please fill up this form.
Firme aquí, por favor -Please sign here
¿Me enseña su pasaporte? - Can you show me your passport?
¿Puedo ver su pasaporte? - Can I see your passport?

Facilities

¿Hay servicio de lavandería? - Is there a laundry?

How long?

Nos quedaremos aquí una noche/unos días/una semana - We'll be here for a night/ a few days/ a week.

Quisiera quedarme una noche más - I'd like to stay an extra night.

¿A qué hora hay que dejar la habitación? - At what time do I have to check out?

¿Puedo dejar mi equipaje aquí? Volveré en dos semanas- Can I leave my bag here? I'll be back in two weeks.

Price

¿Cuánto es por día/ semana? - How much is it per day/ week?
¿Está incluido el desayuno? - Does it include breakfast?
¿Está incluido el IVA? - Does it include VAT?

Complaints

El radiador está estropeado - The room heater is not functioning.
El enchufe está roto - The plug is broken.
Ya estaba estropeado/a - It was already broken.
El grifo no funciona - The tap is not working.

In the hotel

(el) albergue	- youth hostel
(el) hostal	- lodge
cinco estrellas	- five star (maximum category)
(la) temporada alta/baja	- high/low season
(el) equipaje	- luggage
(la) habitación doble	- double room
(la) habitación sencilla	- single room
registrarse	- to check in
recepcionista	- receptionist
(el) botones	- bellboy
(el) ascensor	- lift, elevator
(el) recibidor	- hall, lobby
(el) aparcamiento	- parking
(la) lavandería	- laundry service

(la) piscina	-	swimming-pool
(la) bolsa de viaje	-	travel bag
(la) maleta	-	suitcase
(la) mochila	-	backpack
(el) saco de dormir	-	sleeping bag
(la) luz	-	light
(el) ventilador	-	fan
(el) aire acondicionado	-	air conditioner
(la) calefacción	-	heating
(el) calentador	-	water heater/ geyser
(el) radiador/ calefactor	-	room heater
(la) ducha	-	shower
(la) almohada	-	pillow
(la) manta	-	blanket
(la) percha	-	hanger
(el) jabón	-	soap
(la) basura	-	rubbish
(la) toalla	-	towel
(la) llave	-	key
(la) sábana	-	sheet
(el) papel higénico	-	toilet paper

Condition in requests, orders and invitations: Si + present + imperative or present:

Si quieres, ven conmigo - If you want, come with me.
Si gritas más, me voy - If you shout any more, I will go away.
Si te apetece, puedes venir con nosotros - If you feel like, you can come with us.

Unit 9
AT THE BANK

Ana y Pedro van al banco. Ana quiere cambiar dinero y Pedro quiere abrir una cuenta.

Ana: Buenos días.
Empleado: Buenos días, ¿qué desea?
A: Quisiera cambiar dólares.
E: ¿Cuántos tiene?
A: Ciento cincuenta. ¿A cuánto está el cambio?
E: A ciento cincuenta pesetas el dólar.
A: Muy bien.
E: Firme aquí por favor. Aquí tiene el recibo y el dinero.
A: Muchas gracias. Mi amigo quiere abrir una cuenta de ahorro.
E: Muy bien. Aquí tiene los formularios. ¿Puede rellenarlos?
P: Sí. Ya está.
E: Su pasaporte, por favor.
......
E: Su número de cuenta es AF3300987. Aquí tiene su libreta y puede recoger la tarjeta mañana. Puede pasar por caja a ingresar el dinero.
P: Tengo un cheque.
E: Ah, bueno. Espere un momento, ahora mismo lo hacemos.
P: Muchas gracias.
E: De nada.

Ana and Pedro go to the bank. Ana wants to change money and Pedro wants to open an account.

Ana: Good morning.
Employee: Good morning, how can I help you?
A: I would like to change some dollars.
E: How many?
A: 150 dollars. What is the exchange rate?
E: 150 pesetas a dollar.

A: Very well.
E: Please sign here. Here is the receipt and the money.
A: Thanks a lot. My friend wants to open a savings bank account.
E: OK. Here are the forms. Can you fill them up?
P: Yes, here it is.
E: Your passport, please.

.....

E: Your account number is AF3300987. Here is your passbook and you can take the card tomorrow. You may go to the cash counter to deposit the money.
P: I have a cheque.
E: OK. Please wait a moment, we'll just see to it.
P: Thanks a lot.
E: Welcome.

USEFUL PHRASES ·

Quisiera cambiar dólares/ marcos - I'd like to change some dollars/ marks.
¿Qué moneda tiene? - What currency do you have?
¿A cuánto está (el dólar)? - What is the exchange rate (for dollars)?
¿Me da cambio? - Can you give me change?
Quiero cambiar cheques de viaje - I want to encash some traveller's cheques

¿Puede rellenar este formulario, por favor? - Can you fill this form, please?
¿Puedo ver su pasaporte? - Can I see your passport?
¿Dónde vive? - Where do you live?
¿Dónde se hospeda? - Where are you staying?
Pase por caja - Go to the cash counter
Firme aquí - Sign here
Ahora le atiendo - I'll attend you in a moment

Ya está - It's done
Aquí lo/la tiene - Here it is

Things we do in a bank

abrir una cuenta	- to open an account
ahorrar	- to save
pedir un crédito / préstamo	- to take a loan

pagar a plazos	-	to pay in instalments
ingresar dinero/cheque	-	to deposit money/cheque
sacar dinero	-	to withdraw
invertir	-	to invest
recoger un cheque	-	to collect a cheque
(la) acción	-	share
(la) bolsa	-	stock market
(la) cuenta corriente	-	current account
(la) cuenta de ahorro	-	savings account
(la) libreta, (la) cartilla	-	passbook
(la) caja	-	cash counter
(la) tarjeta de crédito	-	credit card
(el) cajero autómatico	-	automatic teller machine
(el) cajero	-	cashier
(la) cajafuerte	-	safe
(el) recibo	-	receipt
(la) moneda	-	currency
(el) cambio	-	change/exchange
(el) impuesto	-	tax

• **Quisiera** and **me gustaría** are polite forms used while talking to people we don't know or in very formal situations:

Examples:
Quisiera cambiar dinero - I'd like to change some money.
Me gustaría comprar una falda - I'd like to buy a skirt.

See Unit 10 for more detailed use of the Conditional.

Unit 10
SHOPPING

Ana va de compras con Pedro. Están en una tienda de ropa.

Dependiente: Buenos días, señores, ¿qué desean?

A: Buenos días. ¿Puede enseñarme algunas faldas, por favor?

D: ¿De qué talla?

A: Pues, la 40.

D: Tenemos de varios colores. ¿La quiere oscura o clara?

A: ¿Puedo probarme la negra?

D: Por supuesto, allí están los probadores.

......

A: (a Pedro) ¿Cómo me queda?

P: Muy bien.

A: (al dependiente) Me gusta. ¿Qué precio tiene?

D: 8.000 pesetas.

A: Está bien, me la llevo.

D: ¿Quiere pagar con tarjeta o en efectivo?

A: En efectivo. Aquí tiene....

A Pedro le gusta una camiseta y decide comprarla.

P: Mira esta camiseta a cuadros, ¡qué bonita! ¿Te gusta?

A: No mucho. Es de lycra. Me gustan más las de algodón.

P: Es verdad, son más cómodas.

......

P: ¿Qué te parece esta roja?

A: No está mal, pero prefiero la blanca, es más elegante.

P: Me la llevo porque también es más barata.

Ana goes shopping with Pedro. They are in a clothes shop.

Salesman: Good morning, sirs. What would you like?

A: Good morning. Can you show me some skirts, please?

S: What size do you want?

81

A: Well, size 40.
S: We have several colours. Would you like light colours or dark?
A: Can I try the black one?
S: Of course, the trial rooms are there.
A: (to Pedro) Does it suit me?
P: Yes, it is very nice.
A: (to the salesman) I like it. What is the price?
S: 8000 pesetas.
A: It's nice, I'll take it.
S: Would you like to pay with a credit card or in cash?
A: In cash. Here it is....

Pedro likes a T-shirt and decides to buy it.

.....
P: Look at this checked T-shirt, how beautiful it is! Do you like it?
A: Not much. It is made of acrylic. I like cotton ones more.
P: That's true. They are more comfortable.

....
P: What do you think of this red one?
A: Not bad, but I prefer the white one. It's more elegant.
P: I'll take it because it is also cheaper.

USEFUL PHRASES

¿Tienen (faldas escosesas)? - Do you have (Scottish skirts)?
Estoy buscando una camisa azul - I am looking for a blue shirt.
¿Sabe dónde puedo encontrarlo? - Do you know where I can find it?
¿Me enseña otro modelo? - Can you show me another kind?
¿Tiene una talla mayor/ menor? - Do you have a bigger/ smaller size?
¿Qué número? - What size do you want? (for shoes)
¿Qué talla? - What size do you want? (for clothes)
¿Quiere probárselo? - Do you want to try it on?
¿Me queda bien (este vestido)? - Does (this dress) suit me?

¿Tiene garantía? - Does it have a guarantee?
¿Cuánto cuesta/vale (este jersei)? - How much does (this sweater) cost?

¿En tarjeta o en efectivo?- Do you want to pay with a credit card or in cash?

¿Está hecho a mano? - Is it hand-made?
¿Está hecho de ...? Is it made of ....?
¿Se puede lavar a máquina?? - Is is machine washable?
Hay que lavarlo a mano - It must be washed by hand.

VOCABULARY

(la) marca	- mark	(el) escaparate	- shop window
(las) rebajas	- sales	(los) grandes almacenes	- big stores
(el) regalo	- gift		
(el) descuento	- discount		

Clothes

(la) falda	- skirt	(las) medias	- stockings
(la) blusa	- blouse	(los) calcetines	- socks
(los) pantalones	- trousers	(el) abrigo	- coat
(el) vestido	- dress	(la) chaqueta	- jacket
(la) cazadora	- jacket	(el) jersey	- sweater
(el) impermeable	- raincoat	(los) vaqueros	- jeans
(la) camisa	- shirt	(la) ropa interior	- underclothes
(la) corbata	- tie	(el) pijama	- night-suit
(el) traje	- suit	(el) bañador	- swimming trunks
(la) camiseta	- T-shirt	(el) bikini	- bikini

Accessories

(los) zapatos	- shoes	(los) pendientes	- earrings
(las) zapatillas	- sports-shoes	(el) anillo	- ring
(las) sandalias	- sandals	(la) pulsera	- bangle
(las) botas	- boots	(el) collar	- necklace
(el) bolso	- bag	(el) reloj	- watch
(la) cartera	- purse	(el) paraguas	- umbrella
(el) cinturón	- belt	(el) bastón	- walking stick
(el) pañuelo	- scarf	(el) sombrero	- hat
(los) guantes	- gloves	(la) pipa	- pipe

Adjectives with clothes/ accessories

• colours *(see Unit 2)*		caro	- expensive
largo	- long	barato	- cheap
corto	- short	deportivo	- sporty
ancho	- broad/wide	elegante	- elegant
estrecho	- narrow	sucio	- dirty
moderno	- modern	limpio	- clean
clásico	- classic		

See unit 2 for more adjectives

Material

de cuero	- leather	de metal	- metallic
de seda	- silk	de oro	- gold
de algodón	- cotton	de plata	- silver
de lana	- woollen	de madera	- wooden
de lycra	- acrylic, lycra	de plástico	- plastic
de piel	- skin	sintético	- synthetic

Designs/ patterns

liso	- plain	estampado	- printed
a rayas	- striped	a cuadros	- checked
a lunares	- dotted		

Shops

(la) pastelería	-	pastry shop
(la) farmacia	-	chemist shop
(la) droguería	-	store where cleaning materials are sold
(la) perfumería	-	cosmetic shop
(la) mercería	-	hosiery shop
(el) quiosco	-	newsstand
(el) estanco	-	tobacconist
(la) carnicería	-	meat shop
(la) papelería	-	stationary shop
(el) supermercado	-	supermarket
(el) mercado	-	market
(la) tienda de electrodomésticos	-	electronic goods shop

84

(la) peluquería	- barber's shop
(el) salón de belleza	- beauty parlour
(la) tienda de ultramarinos	- grocery shop
(la) librería	- book shop
(la) verdulería	- vegetable and fruit shop

Expressions of surprise/ admiration

- happiness
¡qué bien! - How nice!
¡qué suerte! - How lucky!
enhorabuera / felicidades - Congratulations

- surprise
¡no me digas! - Don't tell me!
¡qué raro! - How strange!

- relief
¡menos mal! - Thank God!

- boredom/irritation
¡qué rollo! - What a bore!
¡qué lío! - What a mess!
¡qué aburrido! - What a bore!

- pity, sadness
¡qué pena! - What a pity!
¡qué triste! - How sad!
¡qué mala suerte! - What bad luck!
¡qué lástima! - What a pity!

GRAMMAR

- ### Verbs which express likes

Verbs like *gustar, encantar, apetecer* are not conjugated according to the subject but according to the object liked, i.e. what appears to be the subject takes the form of the Indirect Object.

me te le nos	gusta este vestido gusta leer novelas
os les	gustan estos bolsos

Since the objects liked are usually in the third person, the third person forms are more often used.

Examples:

Me gusta la ópera

Literally this sentence would translate as *The opera is liked by me* though in English the correct usage is *I like the opera.*

The *me* of **Me gusta** is in fact *gusta a mí* though it is simply written as "me gusta". The a **mí, a ti, etc.** is used only to emphasise or clarify. It is also used to share the liking or express negation in the answer.

- Me gusta esta chaqueta negra.
  A mí también.
  A mí no.
- No me gustan estos calcetines de acrílico.
  A mí tampoco.
  A mí sí.

(A Ana/ a ella) le gusta el pescado.

• **The verb *parecer* - to seem**

The verb *parecer* can also be conjugated according to what appears to be the object of the sentence, in this case the apparent subject is used as the indirect object pronoun:

Below we give the usage of the verb *parecer*

Indirect Object pronoun + parecer + que + subordinate clause
Indirect object pronoun + parecer + adjective

Me, nos Te, os Le, les	**PARECE**	que es peruano que tiene 35 años que se llama Jorge
		interesante, inteligente, divertido,etc.
	PARECEN	serios, simpáticos, tontos, etc.

Examples:

Me parece que Julio es peruano - It seems to me that Julio is Peruvian.

Este hombre me parece muy inteligente - This man seems very intelligent to me.

Estos chicos me parecen muy serios - These boys seem very serious to me.

Parecer can also be used to ask somebody their opinion.

Examples:

¿Qué te parece esta camiseta? - What do you think of this T-shirt?
No está mal/ Es muy bonita. - Its not bad / It is very beautiful.

¿Qué te parece si vamos al cine? - How about going to the cinema?
Bien - OK

Parecerse means to resemble
Me parezco a mi madre - I resemble my mother.

• Verbs like *molestar, doler, interesar, preocupar, divertir, aburrir, fastidiar* can also be used similarly. Here we explain the usage of these verbs with a noun.

Note that when they are used with the relative pronoun (que) + a subordinate clause they take the subjunctive. (See Unit 14)

Examples:

Me molesta el ruido de la calle - The noise from the street disturbs me.
Nos interesa mucho la música clásica - Classical music interests us a lot.

• **The Simple Conditional**

The conjugation of the verbs in the Simple Conditional Tense is as follows:

yo	hablar-**ía**	comer-**ía**	ir-**ía**
tú	hablar-**ías**	comer-**ías**	ir-**ías**
él, ella, usted	hablar-**ía**	comer-**ía**	ir-**ía**
nosotros/as	hablar-**íamos**	comer-**íamos**	ir-**íamos**
vosotros/as	hablar-**íais**	comer-**íais**	ir-**íais**
ellos/as	hablar-**ían**	comer-**ían**	ir-**ían**

The irregular verbs are the same as in the Future Tense. The endings remain the same as that of the regular verbs.

See Appendix 2

Uses of the Simple Conditional

- to express a hypothesis

It is used to express hypothesis about something that has happened in the past. It may be used in a subordinate clause with verbs like *creer, imaginar, suponer* to express a supposition.

Examples:
- ¿Por qué no vino Luis ayer?
- Pues, tendría trabajo/ Me imagino que tendría trabajo.
- Why didn't Luis come yesterday?
- Well, he would have had some work/ I imagine he had some work.

In the above example, both answers have the same meaning.

- **to give advice**

The simple conditional of verbs like *deber* and *tener que* is used to give advice in a very polite manner.

Examples:
Deberías comer más, estás muy delgada - You should eat more, you are very thin.

- **to express a wish using verbs like *gustar***

The simple conditional of the verbs *gustar, encantar, apetecer* (and other verbs that express desire) are used to express wishes, which may or may not be realised.

Examples:
Nos gustaría comprarnos un coche nuevo - We would like to buy a new car.
Querría ir de vacaciones a Nepal - I would like to go on a holiday to Nepal.

- **to politely ask for permission**

The simple conditional of the verb *poder* is used to politely ask permission in very formal situations.

Examples:
¿Podríamos usar vuestro teléfono? - Could we use your telephone?

Comparison

Comparison in Spanish is expressed in the following manner:
1) **más + adjective or adverb + que (more than)**
   menos + adjective or adverb + que (less than)
   tan + adjective + como (as much as)

Examples:
Mi casa es más grande que la de Carlos - My house is bigger than that of Carlos.
Este libro es menos caro que aquél - This book is cheaper than that one.
Ellos no están tan cansados como vosotros - They are not as tired as you are.

2) **verb + más que**
   verb +menos que
   verb + tanto como

Examples:
El pescado me gusta más que la carne - I like fish more than meat.
Yo estudio menos que tú - I study less than you.

Irregular Comparatives:
bueno - mejor
malo - peor
grande - mayor
pequeño - menor

Expressions of surprise

¡Qué + noun + tan + adjective!

Examples:
¡Qué restaurante tan bueno! - What a good restaurant!
¡Qué niño más inteligente! - What an intelligent child!

Gradation and Superlatives

Es	un poco - a little bastante - quite muy - very demasiado - too (much) el/la más - the most	adjective

89

Verb	un poco - a little bastante - quite muy - very demasiado - too (much) el/la más - the most	

Examples:
Es un poco caro - It is a little expensive.
Es demasiado gordo - He is too fat.
Ana es la chica más generosa que conozco - Ana is the most generous girl I know.

Come demasiado - He eats too much.
Habla español muy bien - She speaks Spanish very well.

Superlatives can also be expressed with **ser + ...ísimo/a.**
caro - carísimo/a
guapo - guapísimo/a
grande - grandísimo/a
fácil - facilísimo/a
rico - riquísimo/a
poco - poquísimo/a
mucho - muchísimo/a
bueno - buenísimo/a
malo - malísimo/a

Exercises

1. Complete with *más... (que), menos ... (que), tan ...como, tanto como:*
   a) Este bolso no es ..... bonito ..... aquel.
      Sí, claro, es mucho .... barato .... el otro.
   b) Vamos en tu coche porque es ..... grande que el nuestro.
      Sí, pero es ..... cómodo.
   c) Este piso me ha gustado ..... el otro.
      Sí, pero el otro es ..... caro.
   d) ¿Tú crees que esta habitación es .... pequeña .... la otra?
      Sí, son iguales, pero esta es .... bonita.

2. Fill in the blanks with the correct form of the verbs.
   a) ¿.................... (QUEDAR, a mí) bien estos pantalones?
   b) ¿Qué .... (PARECER, a ti) si me compro una moto?
   c) .... (GUSTAR, a nosotros)más el pescado que la carne.
   d) ¿.................... (PREFERIR, tú) ir al cine o al teatro?
   e) ¿Qué .... (GUSTAR, a ti)más la playa o el monte?,
   f) No .... (GUSTAR, a mí) levantarme temprano.
   g) .... (INTERESAR, a mí) mucho el cine clásico.
   h) .... (MOLESTAR, a nosotros) la música tan alta.
   i) .... (DIVERTIR, a ellos) jugar a cartas.

3. Choose the correct elements from the two columns and make sentences:

A	B
Me parece	que va a llover
Me gustaría	mucho a mi padre
Nos gustan	ir a Paris
Le gusta	jugar a fútbol
Me parezco	los toros

4. Write sentences excusing yourself according to the model:

Example:
¿Quieres venir a tomar unas copas esta noche?
Me gustaría, pero estoy muy cansada (estar muy cansada)

   a) ¿Irás a la fiesta de Beatriz y Gema?
      .... (haber quedado con Julio)

b) A ver si vienes a cenar esta noche a casa...

.... (estar enferma)

c) ¿Por qué no vamos a esquiar a Sierra Nevada?

.... (no saber esquiar)

d) ¿Vendrás este verano a París?

.... (ir a India, ver Taj Mahal).

5. Translate into Spanish:

a) Would you like to go to Spain or do you prefer to stay here?

b) The children are making too much noise. If they disturb you, we can shut the door.

c) You shouldn't work so much. Why don't we go to Manali for a holiday?

Unit 11
TALKING OF THE PAST

Pedro y Ana están hablando.

P: Cuéntame algo de tu vida, Ana.

A: Bueno. Pues, nací en un pueblo pequeño, cerca de Buenos Aires en 1968. Mi padre era médico y mi madre, maestra. Cuando tenía 18 años decidí ir a Buenos Aires a estudiar en la universidad. Yo quería ser médico y mi padre me ayudó como pudo.

P: ¿Por qué te hiciste psiquiatra?

A: Me interesaba mucho estudiar los problemas de la gente.

P: ¿Y cómo es que viniste a Madrid?

A: Pues, un día, cuando iba al hospital donde trabajaba, me encontré con una amiga que había estudiado conmigo en el colegio. Empezamos a hablar y resulta que ella era directora de un hospital aquí y me ofreció este trabajo.

Pedro and Ana are talking.

P: Tell me something about your life, Ana.

A: Well, I was born in a small village near Buenos Aires in 1968. My father was a doctor and my mother, a schoolteacher. When I was eighteen years old I decided to go to Buenos Aires, to study in the university. I wanted to be a doctor and my father helped me as much as he could.

P: Why did you become a psychiatrist?

A: I was very interested in studying the problems of people.

P: How did you happen to come to Madrid?

A: Well, ...one day, while going to the hospital where I used to work, I met a friend who had studied with me in school. We began talking and it turned out that she was the director of a hospital here and offered me this job.

Family

padre/madre	- father/mother	yerno/nuera	- son/daughter-in-law
hijo/a	- son/daughter		
abuelo/a	- grandfather/grandmother	(la) familia	- family
nieto/a	- grandson/daughter	novio/a	- bridegroom/bride boyfriend/girlfriend
hermano/a	- brother/ sister	compañero/a	- colleague
cuñado/a	- brother/sister-in-law	(el) matrimonio	- couple
		marido/mujer	- husband/wife
tío/a	- uncle/aunt	vecino/a	- neighbour
primo/a	- cousin	amigo/a	- friend
sobrino/a	- nephew/niece	(la) pareja	- couple, partner (used for both sexes)
suegro/a	- father/mother-in-law		
		familiar	- relative

Education

(la) enseñanza	- education	(el) cuaderno	- notebook
(el) colegio	- school	(la) libreta	
(el) instituto	- Institute	(la) hoja (de papel)	- sheet (of paper)
(la) universidad	- University		
(el) alumno	- student, pupil	(el) bolígrafo	- pen
maestro/a, profesor/a	- teacher/professor	(el) lápiz	- pencil
		(el) libro	- book
(el) horario	- timetable	(el) diccionario	- dictionary
(la) asignatura	- subject	(la) palabra	- word
(la) química	- Chemistry	(el) significado	- meaning
(la) física	- Physics	(la) ilustración	- picture
(la) historia	- History	diplomado/a	- graduate
(la) lengua	- Language	licenciado/a	- postgraduate
(las) ciencias	- Sciences	doctor/a	- doctor
(la) geografía	- Geography	catedrático/a	- professor
(la) economía	- Economics	(el) diploma	- diploma
(las) matemáticas	- Mathematics	(el) doctorado	- PhD
(el) curso	- course	(la) tesis	- thesis
(la) clase	- classroom		
(el) examen	- exam	aprender	- to learn
(las) notas	- marks	aprobar	- to pass an exam

comprender/	- to understand	explicar	- to explain
entender		leer	- to read
contar	- to count	preguntar	- to ask
deletrear	- to spell out	repetir	- to repeat
enseñar	- to teach	suspender	- to fail
escribir	- to write	traducir	- to translate

GRAMMAR

• The Past Imperfect Tense

The Past Imperfect Tense is conjugated in the following manner:

hablar	comer	vivir
habl-**aba**	com-**ía**	viv-**ía**
habl-**abas**	com-**ías**	viv-**ías**
habl-**aba**	com-**ía**	viv-**ía**
habl-**ábamos**	com-**íamos**	viv-**íamos**
habl-**abais**	com-**íais**	viv-**íais**
habl-**aban**	com-**ían**	viv-**ían**

This tense is used
1. to express a continuous action or state in the past.

Examples:
Cuando *era* pequeño, *vivía* en el pueblo - When I was small I used to live in the village.
Cuando *tenía* 10 años *estudiaba* en un colegio grande - When I was ten years old, I used to study in a big school.

2. to express a repeated or customary action or state in the past

Examples:
Siempre *jugaba* con los mismos amigos - I always used to play with the same friends.
Todos los días *íbamos* al parque - We used to go to the park everyday.

95

• The Past Indefinite Tense

The Past Indefinite Tense is conjugated in the following way:

hablar	comer	vivir
habl-**é**	com-**í**	viv-**í**
habl-**aste**	com-**iste**	viv-**iste**
habl-**ó**	com-**ió**	viv-**ió**
habl-**amos**	com-**imos**	viv-**imos**
habl-**asteis**	com-**isteis**	viv-**isteis**
habl-**aron**	com-**ieron**	viv-**ieron**

See Appendix 2 for irregular verb patterns.

It is used with the following time sequences:
Ayer - yesterday
Anteayer - day before yesterday
Anoche - last night
Antenoche - night before last
El otro día …- the other day
El mes/ verano/ año pasado - last month/ summer/ year
La semana pasada etc. - last week, etc.

1. To express a concrete action which has occured at a concrete moment in the past.
   Ayer *hablé* con mi amiga por teléfono - Yesterday I spoke to my friend on the telephone.
   Anoche *fui* al cine - Yesterday I went to the movies.
   El otro día *vi* a Ana en el mercado - The other day I saw Ana in the market.

2. In relation to the Imperfect tense to narrate a particular event in the past tense.
   Cuando *iba* al colegio *vi* a tu madre - When I was going to school, I saw your mother.
   El otro día, cuando *hablaba* con mis amigas, me *llamó* mi padre - The other day, when I was talking to my friends, my father called me.
   Here, the action that interrupts is used in the Indefinite Tense whereas the verb which expresses a situation in the past is used in the Imperfect.

96

• The Past Continuous Tense

The Past Continuous Tense in Spanish is used with the verb **estar** in the Imperfect Tense with the Gerund.

estaba
estabas
estaba   + hablando/ comiendo/ escribiendo
estábamos
estabais
estaban

Examples:
Estábamos comiendo cuando sonó el teléfono - We were eating when the telephone rang.

Exercises

1. Fill in the blanks with the verb in the *Past Imperfect* or *Past Indefinite* tense:

   Una noche, mientras Miguel .... (dormir), su madre .... (ver) la televisión. De repente, ... (oir) un ruido muy extraño y ...... (ir) a la habitación para ver que .... (pasar). ....(Encontrar) a su hijo durmiendo tranquilamente. .... (Volver) al salón y ...... (seguir) viendo la televisión.

2. Complete the sentences using the *Past Imperfect* or the *Present tense*:

   a) Antes no .... (trabajar, yo) e .... (ir, yo) a correr todos los días. Ahora .... (trabajar, yo) y .... (estar, yo) muy ocupado.
   b) Antes .... (levantarse, ella) muy temprano, ahora .... (estar) de vacaciones y .... (levantarse) a las doce.
   c) En 1987 nosotros .... (vivir) en Caracas, ahora .... (vivir, nosotros) en La Paz.
   d) Cuando ...... (ser, yo) estudiante, ... (hacer, yo) deporte, pero desde que trabajo no ...... (poder, yo).
   e) Cuando .... (tener, tú) trece años .... (bañarse, tú) en el río todos los días.

3. Choose the action from column A and the circumstance from column B and make sentences as in the example:
   El jueves pasado estuve en México D.F. porque tenía una reunión muy importante.

A	B
ir al dentista (el martes pasado, yo)	tener mucho dolor de muelas
quedarse en casa (el lunes pasado, yo)	estar muy cansado
no ir al gimnasio (la semana pasada, Mario)	doler mucho el pie
ir de excursión (el fin de semana pasado, nosotros)	hacer muy buen tiempo

Unit 12
ENTERTAINMENT

Ana y Pedro miran la cartelera.

A: ¿Te apetece ver una película?

P: Sí, vale. *Fresa y chocolate* está muy bien, la ponen en sesión de madrugada aquí al lado.

A: Es que es muy tarde. ¿Por qué no vamos al teatro? Esta obra parece interesante.

P: Bueno, ¿puedes ir a por las entradas?

A: Sí, claro

P: ¡Mira! El domingo juega el Barça y el Real Madrid. ¿Te gustaría ir?

A: No, no me gusta el fútbol. Además será muy caro.

Juan and Pedro are looking at the programme.

A: Do you feel like seeing a film?

P: Yes, OK. *Fresa y chocolate* is very good, it is running in the late night show in the theatre nearby.

A: It's very late. Why don't we go to the theatre? This play seems interesting.

P: OK, can you go for the tickets?

A: Yes, of course.

P: Look, Barça and Real Madrid are playing on Sunday. Would you like to go?

A: No, I don't like football. Moreover, it will be very expensive.

USEFUL PHRASES

¿Tienes una cartelera?- Do you have a programme?

¿Puedes recomendarme un(a) buen(a) (película)?- Can you recommend a good (film)?

¿Hay algún (ballet) en algún sitio?- Is there a (ballet) on somewhere?

99

¿Cuándo empieza?- When does it start?
¿Cuándo acaba?- When does it end?
¿Hay sitio para (esta noche)?- Are there any seats for (tonight)?

¿Cuánto cuesta una butaca?- How much are the seats?
Una entrada, por favor- One ticket, please
Quería reservar (tres) entradas para (el sábado por la noche)- I'd
like to reserve (three) tickets for (Saturday night).

(el) cine	- cinema
(el) teatro	- theatre
(el) ballet	- ballet
(la) fila	- row
(la) sesión de tarde/noche/ madrugada	- evening/ night/ late night show
(el) descanso/ (el) intermedio	- interval
(la) cola	- queue
(la) taquilla	- box office

Cinema and theatre

¿Qué película ponen hoy en el cine?- What film is on today?
¿La película es doblada/en versión original subtitulada? Is the film
dubbed/subtitled?

¿Qué obra hacen en el teatro (Eslava)?- What is playing at the
(Eslava) Theatre?
¿Quién es el autor?- Who is the playwright?

(la) película	- film/movie	guionista	- screenplay writer
(la) pantalla	- screen	actor/ actriz	- actor/ actress
(los) dibujos animados	- cartoons	(el) decorado	- scenery
(el) anuncio publicitario	- advertisement	(la) banda sonora	- soundtrack
acomodador	- usher	(el) próximo estreno	- new release
director	- film maker		

100

Music

¿Qué orquesta/grupo está tocando?- Which orchestra/band is playing?

¿Qué están tocando?- What are they playing?

¿Quién es el/a director(a)/solista?- Who is the conductor/soloist?

¿Son conocidos?- Are they popular?

cantante	- singer	(el) concierto	- rock/ jazz concert
(la) orquesta	- orchestra	de rock/ jazz	
(el) violín	- violin	(la) discoteca	- discothèque
(el) piano	- piano	(el) altavoz	- loudspeaker
(la) guitarra	- guitar	(el) micrófono	- microphone
(la) batería	- drums		

Sports

¿Hay algún (partido de fútbol) (este sábado)? - Is there any (football match) (this Saturday)?

¿Qué equipos están jugando? - Which teams are playing?

¿Puedes conseguirme una entrada? - Can you get me a ticket?

¿Necesito ser miembro? - Do I need to be a member? (in a club)

¿Puedo alquilar (un caballo)? - Can I hire (a horse)?

¿Puedo recibir algunas clases? - Can I take some lessons?

¿Cuánto es por día/vuelta/hora? - What is the charge per day/round/hour?

¿Puedo unirme a vosotros?- Can I join in?

(el) fútbol	- football	(la) portería	- goal line
(el) tenis	- tennis	portero	- goalkeeper
(el) baloncesto	- basketball	(la) red	- net
(el) atletismo	- athletics	(el) balón/ (la)	- ball
(la) natación	- swimming	pelota	
(la) gimnasia	- gymnastics	(la) raqueta	- racket
(el) judo	- judo	árbitro	- referee
(el) marcador	- scoreboard	juez	- umpire
(el) equipo	- team	(la) línea	- line
(los) espectadores	- spectators	ganar	- to win
(la) cancha/	- court	perder	- to lose
(la) pista		empatar	- to equalize
(el) campo	- pitch	nadar	- to swim

correr	- to run	(la) plaza de toros	- bullring
navegar	- to sail	(la) corrida	- bullfight
jugar (a)	- to play	torero	- bullfighter

Having fun

bailar	- to dance	jugar al bingo	- to play bingo
tomar copas	- to have a drink	jugar a las cartas	- to play cards
tomar el aperitivo	- to have an aperitif		

The sea, the mountains and the countryside.

(el) paisaje-landscape		(la) montaña	- mountain
(el/la) mar	- sea	(el) pico	- peak
(la) isla	- island	(el) monte	- mount
(la) costa	- coast	(el) valle	- valley
(la) playa	- beach	(la) aldea	- hamlet
(las) rocas	- rocks	(el) pueblo	- village
(la) ola	- wave	(la) oveja	- sheep
(la) orilla	- shore / bank	(el) caballo	- horse
(la) arena	- sand	(el) toro	- bull
(el) bosque	- wood	(la) vaca	- cow
(el) campo	- countryside	(el) pájaro	- bird
(el) árbol	- tree	gato/a	- cat
(la) flor	- flower	perro/a	- dog
(la) hierba	- grass	cerdo/a	- pig
(la) planta	- plant	burro/a	- donkey
(el) lago	- lake	(la) mosca	- fly
(el) río	- river	(el) mosquito	- mosquito
(la) tierra	- land	(la) mariposa	- butterfly

Politics

(la) monarquía	- monarchy
(la) democracia	- democracy
(la) dictadura	- dictatorship
(el) rey, (la) reina	- king, queen
diputado/a, senador/a	- member of parliament, senator
presidente	- President, Prime Minister.

(el) parlamento	-	Parliament
(el) consejo de ministros	-	council of ministers
(el) partido político	-	political party
votar	-	to vote
(las) elecciones	-	elections
(el) sindicato	-	trade union
(la) huelga	-	strike
comunista	-	communist
centro	-	centrist
socialista	-	socialist
conservador	-	conservative
(la) seguridad social	-	social security
(el) servicio militar	-	military service
(la) justicia	-	judiciary
ser de izquierdas/ derechas	-	to be a leftist/rightist
pertenecer a un partido político	-	to belong to a political party

Mass media

(la) televisión	-	television
(la) radio	-	radio
(el) informativo	-	newscast
(el) programa de debate	-	debate programme
(el) programa musical	-	musical programme
(el) programa deportivo	-	sports programme
(el) anuncio	-	advertisement
(la) publicidad	-	advertising
presentador/a	-	announcer
locutor/a	-	newscaster
encender la televisión	-	to turn on the TV
apagar la televisión	-	to turn off the TV
(la) prensa	-	press
(el) periódico	-	newspaper
(los) titulares	-	headlines
(el) artículo	-	article
(la) foto	-	photo
(la) revista	-	magazine
(el) tebeo	-	comic

GRAMMAR

- **to express cause and consequence**

The following expressions may be used to express cause:
Por eso - That's why
Por lo tanto - Therefore
Asi que - So, thus
O sea que - Or, in other words
Es que - It's just that

The expressions given below express consequence:
porque - because
puesto que - As a result
Ya que - because
Cómo es que - How is is that

Unit 13
HEALTH

Ana está enferma y va a una clínica.

Ana: Quisiera ver al doctor Carlos Navarro, si es posible.

Enfermera: Lo siento, está ocupado. ¿Tenía cita?

A: No, pero me encuentro muy mal.

E: Ahora mismo le aviso.

....

Doctor: ¿Qué le pasa?

A: Tengo fiebre alta, temblores y me duele el estómago.

Dr.: ¿Le ha sentado algo mal?

A: No, he comido como siempre y llevo dos días así.

Dr.: Tiene 38º C de fiebre. Veamos la tensión...

A: La tengo normalmente un poco baja.

Dr.: Voy a hacerle unos análisis y un chequeo general.

En casa

Pedro: ¿Sabes que Luis se ha roto el brazo?

Ana: ¿Cómo?

P: Jugando a fútbol con sus hijos.

Ana is unwell and she goes to a clinic.

Ana: I would like to see Dr. Carlos Navarro, if it is possible.

Nurse: I'm sorry, but he's busy. Do you have an appointment?

A: No, but I am very ill.

N: I'll inform him right away.

....

Doctor: What's the matter?

A: I have high fever, shivering and my stomach is aching.

Dr: Is it something you've eaten?

Ana: No, I have eaten as usual and I am like this for the past two days.

Dr: Your temperature is 38º C. Let's see your pressure.

A: It's usually a little low.

Dr: I'm going to do some tests and a general check-up.

At home

Pedro: Do you know Luis has broken his arm?

Ana: How did it happen?

P: While playing football with his sons.

USEFUL PHRASES

Para visitar al médico- To visit the doctor

¿Dónde puedo encontrar un médico/dentista?- Where can I find a doctor/dentist?

¿Cuál es el horario de consulta?- What are the consulting hours?

¿Puede el médico venir a verme aquí?- Could the doctor come to see me here?

¿Puedo coger cita para (el miércoles) (por la mañana)?- Can I take an appoiment for (Wednesday morning)?

Es urgente- It is urgent

Tengo una cita (con el Dr. Pardo) - I have an appointment (with Dr.Pardo)

Ahora mismo le aviso - I will inform him rightaway.

¿Qué te/le pasa? - What's the matter?

Estoy enfermo/a - I am sick

Estoy resfriado/a - I have a cold

Estoy nervioso/a - I am nervous

Tengo fiebre - I have fever

Tengo una insolación - I have a sunstroke

Tengo el estómago revuelto - My stomach is upset

Tengo faringitis - I have a sore throat

Tengo el pie hinchado - I have a swollen foot

Tengo tortículis - I have a stiff neck

Tengo una herida en la mano - I have a wound in my hand

Tengo asma - I have asthma

Me duele (el estómago) - I have a (stomach ache)

Me duele aquí - It hurts here

Me ha sentado mal la comida - The food has not suited me

He vomitado varias veces - I have vomited several times

No me encuentro bien - I am not feeling well
No puedo dormir - I can't sleep
Me he roto el brazo - I have broken (fractured) my arm
Me he torcido el tobillo/la muñeca - I have sprained my ankle/wrist
Me he dado un golpe (en la cabeza) - I have banged (my head)
Me he quemado (la mano) - I have burnt (my hand)
Me he cortado (en el pie) - I have cut (my foot)
Me he doblado la rodilla - I have twisted my knee
Me ha picado una medusa/un mosquito/una avispa - I have been stung by a jellyfish/a mosquito/ a wasp
Soy alérgico/a a (la penicilina) - I am allergic (to penicillin)
Sufro del corazón - I have a heart condition
Tuve un ataque al corazón (hace 2 años) - I had a heart attack (two years ago)
Soy diabético/a - I am diabetic
Soy hipertenso/a - I have high blood pressure
Soy epiléptico/a - I am epileptic
Estoy embarazada/en estado - I am pregnant
Tengo el periodo - I have the period
Tomo la píldora - I am on the pill
Voy a desmayarme - I am going to faint
Necesito unos análisis - I need some tests
Necesito un chequeo general - I need a complete check-up
Llevo así (dos) semanas - I have been like this for (two) weeks

¡No me toques! ¡Me duele! - Don't touch... it's painful!

Consejos médicos - Medical advice

Parece enfermo/a - You look ill
¿Le duele? - Does it hurt?
¿Desde cuándo se siente así? - How long have you been feeling like this?
¿Es la primera vez que le pasa esto? - Is this the first time you have had this?
¿Está tomando alguna otra medicina? - Are you taking any other medicines?
¿Es alérgico a algo? - Are you allergic to anything?
¿Está vacunado contra (el tétanos)? - Have you been vaccinated against (tetanus)?
¿Ha perdido el apetito? - Have you lost your appetite?

No es nada serio- It isn't too serious
No se preocupe - Don't worry
Descanse- Take rest
Cuídese- Look after yourself
Debe quedarse en cama- You must stay in bed
Voy a enviarle al hospital para hacerle una radiografía- I'm going
to send you to hospital to have an X-ray taken
Le recomiendo...- I recommend ...
Debe tomar...- You must take...
Tome calmantes/analgésicos tres veces al día- Take
tranquilizers/ pain-killers three times a day
Le aconsejo que coma muy poco- I advice you to eat very little
Le aconsejo que beba sólo agua- I advice you to drink only water
Se sentirá pronto mejor- You will soon feel better

antes/después de las comidas- before/after meals
durante tres días- for three days

En la farmacia - At the chemist shop

¿Dónde está la farmacia (de guardia) más cercana?- Where is the
nearest (all-night) pharmacy?
¿A qué hora abren/cierran la farmacia?- What time does the
pharmacy open/close?

¿Puede hacer esta receta (para mí)?- Can you make this
prescription (for me)?
¿Puedo comprarlo sin receta?- Can I get it without a prescription?
¿Me da (un jarabe para la tos), por favor?- Can I have (a cough
syrup), please?

¿Cuánto debo tomar?- How much should I take?
¿Cada cuánto debo tomarlo?- How often should I take it?
¿Es conveniente para niños?- Is it suitable for children?

VOCABULARY
Hospital - Hospital

médico/a	- doctor	(la) medicina	- medicine
enfermero/a	- nurse	(la) sala	- ward
enfermo/a	- ill	(la) cama	- bed
herido/a	- injured	(la) camilla	- stretcher
minusválido	- handicapped	(el) dolor	- pain

(la) escayola	- plaster	(las) urgencias	- emergency
(el) termómetro	- thermometer	(el) ambulancia	- ambulance
(la) venda	- bandage	(la) sirena	- siren/alarm
(la) inyección	- injection		

Medicamentos - Medication

(el) jarabe	- syrup	(el) repelente	- insect repellent
(la) pastilla	- tablet	de insectos	
(la) píldora	- pill	(los) analgésicos	- painkillers
(la) crema	- antiseptic	(las) vitaminas	- vitamin tablets
antiséptica	cream	(la) medicina	- medicine
(la) aspirina	- (soluble)aspirin		
(efervescente)			

Quejas - Complaints

(el) asma	- asthma	(la) hepatitis	- hepatitis
(el) ataque de	- heart attack	(la) malaria	- malaria
corazón		(la) picadura de	- insect bite
(el) calambre	- cramp	insecto	
(el) cáncer	- cancer	(la) pneumonia	- pneumonia
(el) cólera	- cholera	(la) quemadura	- sunburn
(el) estreñimiento	- constipation	solar	
(el) mareo	- travel sickness	(la) rabia	- rabies
(el) SIDA	- AIDS	(la) resaca	- hangover
(la) anemia	- anaemia	(la) torcedura	- sprain
(la) artritis	- arthritis	(la) tos	- cough
(la) diabetes	- diabetes	(la) varicela	- measles
(la) diarrea	- diarrhoea	(la) viruela	- chicken-pox
(la) gripe	- influenza	(los) hemorroides	- haemorrhoids/
(la) hemorragia	- haemorrhage		piles

Partes del cuerpo - Parts of the body

(la) barbilla	- chin	(el) corazón	- heart
(la) boca	- mouth	(el) cuerpo	- body
(el) brazo	- arm	(el) dedo	- finger
(la) cabeza	- head	(el) diente	- tooth
(la) cara	- face	(la) espalda	- back
(el) codo	- elbow	(el) estómago	- stomach

(la) frente	- forehead	(el) pecho	- chest
(la) garganta	- throat	(el) pie	- foot
(el) hombro	- shoulder	(la) piel	- skin
(los) labios	- lips	(la) pierna	- leg
(la) lengua	- tongue	(el) pulgar	- thumb
(la) mano	- hand	(el) pulmón	- lung
(la) mejilla	- cheek	(la) rodilla	- knee
(el) muslo	- thigh	(la) sangre	- blood
(la) nariz	- nose	(el) tobillo	- ankle
(el) ojo	- eye	(la) uña	- nail
(el) oído	- ear		

110

Unit 14
TROUBLES

Pedro se encuentra a una persona herida en la calle

P: ¡Socorro! ¡Ayuda por favor!

X: ¿Qué pasa chico?

P: Hay un hombre herido en aquella acera, parece que le han pegado un tiro. Por favor llame a una ambulancia inmediatamente, está perdiendo mucha sangre.

X: Llame usted, mientras tanto yo voy a verlo, soy médico.

Pedro sees a wounded person on the street.

P: Help! Please help us.

X: What's the matter?

P: There is a wounded man on the pavement, it seems he has been shot. Please call an ambulance immediately, he is bleeding a lot.

X: You call the ambulance, while I'll go and look at him. I'm a doctor.

Pedro ha perdido su cartera.

P: Me han robado la cartera con el pasaporte, mis tarjetas de crédito, la credencial de periodista y unas 12.000 pesetas más o menos.

Sr.: ¿Cómo ha sucedido?

P: Salía de mi casa de camino a la oficina, y de repente noté que me tiraban de la bolsa, grité pero ya era demasiado tarde. El ladrón salió corriendo.

Pedro has lost his bag.

P: I have been robbed of my purse with my passport, credit cards, my identity card and about 12,000 pesetas.

Sr.: How did it happen?

111

P: I was on my way to the office from home, and suddenly I felt that someone was pulling at my bag. I shouted but it was too late. The thief ran away.

Hay gente en la calle esperando a que abran una tienda, lleva varios días cerrada.

A: ¿Verdad que abren a las siete? ¡Pues está cerrado! ¡Tendrían que avisar un día antes!

B: Deberían poner un cartel con un teléfono de urgencia. ¡No hay derecho!

C: Sí, ¡ya está bien! No puede ser que cada vez que les apetezca nos dejen en la calle. Estoy harto.

There are people in the street waiting for a shop to open, which has been closed for many days

A: Don't they open at six? Well, it's still closed. They should inform a day in advance.

B: They should put a notice with an emergency telephone number. It's not fair.

C: Yes, that's right. It is not fair to leave us out in the street whenever they feel like. I am fed up.

Pedro ha roto sin querer un frasco de perfume de Ana.

P: Siento muchísimo lo que ha ocurrido.

A: No te preocupes, en parte ha sido culpa mía, no debería haberlo dejado sobre la mesa.

P: Perdona que tampoco te dijese nada, tenía miedo que te enfadases conmigo.

Pedro has unknowingly broken Ana's perfume.

P: I'm sorry for what has happened.

A: Don't worry. It's partly my fault, I shouldn't have left it on the table.

P: Sorry for not mentioning anything. I was scared that you'd get angry with me.

Pedro quiere arreglar su ordenador portátil urgentemente

P: ¿Podrían arreglármelo ahora mismo?

Sr.: Lo siento hasta la semana que viene no podrá ser, de todas formas en cuanto lo tenga le aviso por teléfono.

P: Lo necesitaba enseguida, para hoy a las 5.

Sr.: Puede llevarlo a Electrodomésticos Pineda, lo arreglan inmediatamente y lo hacen muy bien sólo que es un poco caro.

P: Muchas gracias, es urgente.

Pedro wants to get his laptop repaired urgently

P: Can you repair it right away?

M: I'm sorry, it's not possible until next week. In any case, I'll inform you by telephone as soon as it is ready.

P: I need it immediately, at five this evening.

M: You can take it to Pineda Electrodomestics, they repair things immediately and do it well. But they are a little expensive.

P: Thank you, it is urgent.

Cómo expresar insatisfacción / Expressing dissatisfaction

Estar harto/a de + noun or verb in infinitive - to be fed up of something

Examples:

Estoy harto de los médicos - I am fed of doctors.

Estoy harto de hablar de este tema - I am fed up of talking about this topic

No soporto (a + person/ noun)/ verb in infinitive - I can't bear someone/something

Examples:

No soporto a Juan - I can't tolerate Juan

Me molesta/n or fastidia/n + noun or verb in infinitive - someone/ something disturbs/ irritates me

Examples:

Me fastidian los atascos - Traffic jams irritate me.

Me molesta ese ruido - That noise disturbs me.

• The Compound Tenses

Past Perfect Tense

The Past Perfect Tense is used to indicate an action in the past with respect to the past tense. It is a compound tense formed with the **Past Imperfect Tense** of the verb **haber** and the **Past Participle**.

```
Había
Habías
Había
Habíamos  + hablado/ comido/ bebido
Habíais
Habían
```

Examples:

Cuando llegó la policía al banco, los ladrones ya *se habían escapado* - When the police reached the bank, the theives had already escaped

Future Perfect Tense

While the Simple Future Tense expresses actions which will take place in the future, the Future Perfect Tense is used to express the probability of something happening in the future. It is a compound tense formed with the **Future Tense** of the verb **haber** and the **Past Participle**.

```
Habré
Habrás
Habrá
Habremos  + hablado/ comido/ bebido
Habréis
Habrán
```

Examples:

Enrique *habrá perdido* el tren. - Henry shall have missed the train

Compound conditional

See Unit 15 for use of this tense.

```
Habría
Habrías
Habría
Habríamos + hablado/ comido/ bebido
Habríais
Habrían
```

114

Impersonality and Passive Voice

Impersonality can be expressed in the following ways:

1. SE + 3rd person singular or plural forms of the verb is used when the agent of the verb is not important.
   Este edificio se empezó a construir en 1945. - The construction of this building began in 1945.
   Se habla español aquí - Spanish is spoken here.

2. The verb **ser in the Present Perfect or Past Indefinite + Past Participle** also expresses passive voice. The preposition **por** identifies the agent of the verb.

El Quijote fue escrito por Cervantes - *El Quijote* was written by Cervantes.
Este edificio ha sido reconstruido este año - This building has been reconstructed this year.

Subjunctive: Past and Present

SUBJUNCTIVE

Present			Past		
hablar	**comer**	**vivir**	**hablar**	**comer**	**vivir**
hable	coma	viva	hablara, hablase	comiera, comiese	viviera, viviese
hables	comas	vivas	hablaras, hablases	comieras, comieses	vivieras, vivieses
hable	coma	viva	hablara, hablase	comiera, comiese	viviera, viviese
hablemos	comamos	vivamos	habláramos, hablásemos	comiéramos, comiésemos	viviéramos, viviésemos
habléis	comáis	viváis	hablarais, hablaseis	comierais, comieseis	vivierais, vivieseis
hablen	coman	vivan	hablaran, hablasen	comieran, comiesen	vivieran, viviesen

Present Perfect Subjunctive

HAYA
HAYAS
HAYA
HAYAMOS + hablado/ comido/ bebido
HAYÁIS
HAYAN

Past Perfect Subjunctive

HUBIERA, HUBIESE
HUBIERAS, HUBIESES
HUBIERA, HUBIESE
HUBIÉRAMOS/ HUBIÉSEMOS + hablado/ comido/ bebido
HUBIERAIS, HUBIESEIS
HUBIERAN, HUBIESEN

Note : The Present Subjunctive Tense preserves all the irregularities of the Present Indicative and the Past Subjunctive those of the Past Indefinite Tense.

The Subjunctive is used primarily in the following cases. The difference in use of the Present and the Past Subjunctive depends on the tense of the main clause. If the main clause is in the Present Tense, the Present Subjunctive is used and similarly the Past, except in few cases where special mention is made of the particular exception. The Subjunctive is usually used only when the subject of the main and subordinate clauses are not the same. The following is not an exhaustive list and the user may consult a grammar for more specific information:

- **In subordinate clauses:**

When the main clause expresses a feeling or sentiment the Subjunctive is used. In the case of Impersonal verb forms like *Es raro que* the Indicative may be used to make a general statement.

a) Surprise or worry:
   ¡Que raro/extraño que + Subjunctive!
   Es raro/extraño que + Subjunctive
   Tengo miedo de que + Subjuncive
   Me sorprende que + Subjunctive
   Es imposible/increíble que + Subjunctive
   Es alucinante que + Subjunctive

b) Pity or sadness:
   ¡Qué pena/lástima que + Subjunctive!
   Es una pena/lástima que + Subjunctive
   Lo siento mucho que + Subjunctive

c) Happiness
   Me alegro (mucho) de que + Subjunctive
   ¡Qué bien que + Subjunctive!

d) Thanks
   Le agradezco que + Subjunctive

When the main verb expresses an intention to influence the subordinate action. Note that when the subject is the same, the infinitive is used.

a) With verbs expressing desire, order, request, advice, like *querer, pedir, decir, mandar, exigir, rogar, aconsejar, etc.*
   Quiero que vengas (tú) inmediatamente.
   Te ruego que no se lo digas.

But when the subject is the same, the Infinitive is used :
Quiero ir a España este año.

b) With verbs expressing belief or opinion in the negative like
    pensar, creer, opinar
    No creo que vengan hoy.
    No pensamos que Manuel sepa la verdad.

c) With verbs that express obligation
    Es necesario que vengas
    No hace falta que me traigas un regalo.

d) With verbs expressing doubt like *dudar*
    Dudamos que vengan tan temprano.

When requesting and granting permission

Te/le/os/les importa/molesta que + Present Subjunctive
(requesting permission)
¿Te importa que baje el volúmen?.

In the following case though the Indicative mood is used:
Te/le/os/les importa/ molesta si + Present Indicative (requesting
permission): ¿Os molesta si fumo?
Te/le/os/les importa/molesta + Infinitive (asking to somebody to
do something): ¿Le importa cerrar la puerta?

Expressing wishes

¡Qué + Present Subjuntive!: ¡Qué te vaya bien todo!
Espero que + Present Subjuntive: ¡Espero que se mejore!
¡Ojalá (que) + Subjunctive: ¡Ojalá llueva en Santo Domingo!

When expressing doubt, probability or hypotheses, the Indicative or the Subjunctive may be used as the case may be:

Es posible/ probable que + Subjunctive: Es posible que venga
mañana.
Puede ser que + Present or Present Perfect Subjunctive: Puede
ser que se hayan quedado sin gasolina.
Quizás + Present or Present Perfect Subjunctive or Indicative:
Quizás llame/llamará más tarde.

Tal vez + Present or Present Perfect Subjunctive or Indicative: Tal vez irá/vaya el próximo verano.
Probablemente/ Posiblemente + Indicative or Subjuntive
A lo mejor + Indicative: A lo mejor nieva este año.
Seguramente + Indicative: Seguramente volverá el lunes.
Seguro que + Indicative: Seguro que has trabajado todo el día.

When expressing an evidence or truth the Indicative Mood is used, in the negative forms Subjunctive is used:

No es cierto que + Subjunctive
No es verdad que + Subjunctive
No es evidente que + Subjunctive
No está demostrado que + Subjunctive
No está claro que + Subjunctive

• **In Temporal Clauses**

AUNQUE = Even though

We use the Subjunctive with *aunque* when we don't have enough information about something, or when we are not sure if something will happen in the future, or when we want to express disagreement:

Aunque no te apetezca, tienes que venir.
El año que viene, aunque no tenga dinero, pienso ir a Nueva York.

HASTA = until

When *hasta* refers to a future action, the Subjunctive Mood is used. When the reference is to a past action, the Indicative Mood is used:
No me iré hasta que no venga Marcos.
Estuve esperando hasta que Raquel llegó.

If the subject is the same in both the clauses there are two possibilities:

a) Hasta + Infinitive/Noun
   Me quedaré (yo) en la India hasta casarme(yo)
   Me quedaré (yo) en la India hasta el día de mi boda.

b) Hasta + Subjunctive
   Me quedaré (yo)en la India hasta que me case (yo).

CUANDO = when

When *cuando* refers to the future or a future action, it is used with the Subjunctive Mood:

Por favor, llamadme por teléfono cuando lleguen María y Carmen.

ANTES DE (QUE) = before
DESPUÉS DE (QUE) = after

Antes (de) que and *después de que* are used with Subjunctive when the subjects are different.
Díselo (tú) antes de que venga (él).
Antes (de) and *después (de)* are used with the Infinitive when the subjects are the same.
Antes de irte (tú) a vivir a Brasil, deberías (tú) consultárselo a tus padres.

MIENTRAS = as long as

When *mientras* refers to the future, Subjunctive Mood is used; if it a habitual action or refers to the past, Indicative Mood is used:
Mientras vivas allí, escríbenos.
Mientras estaba aparcando, me pusieron una multa.

- **With particles expressing finality or conditions:**
PARA QUE = so that

Te traigo este periódico para que me lo leas.
When the subject is the same we use *para + infinitive*.
Estudio español para poder ir a España.

SI = if

Si + Indicative is used when the condition is likely to be fulfilled:
Si hace sol, iremos a la playa.
Si quieres el libro, ven a mi casa.

Si is used with Past Subjunctive when the condition is unlikely to be fulfilled or to express an unrealisable wish/desire:
Si hiciera sol, iríamos a la playa.
Si fuera el presidente del país, cambiaría algunas leyes.

OTHER PARTICLES

These particles can be used with the Present or the Past Subjunctive. If the main clause is in the Present Tense, the Present Subjunctive is used and if the main clause is in the Past Tense, the Past Subjunctive is used:
a)   con tal (de) que
b)   siempre que
c)   siempre y cuando
d)   en el caso de
e)   excepto que
· f)   salvo que
g)   a no ser que

Examples:
Te doy el libro con tal de que me lo devuelvas mañana.
Os di las llaves de mi casa con tal de que no os quedarais allí más de una semana.

INDIRECT SPEECH

When a dialogue is put into indirect speech, it is usually introduced by the verb decir. Some of the changes that take place:

•   Change of first person to third.

•   Change in adverbs of time and place:
"No me voy" (yo) → Dice que no se va (él).
"Mi madre se ha ido" → Dice que su madre se ha ido.
"Llevo mucho tiempo aquí" → Dice que lleva mucho tiempo allí.
"Voy ahora" → Dice que va ahora
                    Dijo que iba entonces

•   If a question is to be put into Indirect Speech there are two possibilities:
If there is an interogative pronoun, then the *que* is dropped.
If there is no interogative pronoun *si* is used.

Examples :
¿Dónde víves? - Pregunta (que) dónde vives.
¿ Trabajas aquí? - Pregunta si trabaja allí.

- Changes in tenses and verb forms as follows:

When the main clause is in the Present Tense	
¿QUÉ DICE?	
Direct Speech **Verb in Indicative**	**Indirect Speech** **Verb in Indicative**
Como demasiado	Dice que come demasiado
Tenía mucha hambre	...tenía mucha hambre
Fui a Pekín	...fue a Pekín
He viajado poco	...ha viajado poco
No iré al cine	...no irá al cine
Habré cantado más de ocho canciones	...habrá cantado más de ocho canciones
Llegaría a las cinco	...llegaría a las cinco
Habría ganado suficiente	...habría ganado suficiente
Direct Speech **Verb in Imperative**	**Indirect Speech** **Verb in Present Subjunctive**
Cállate y no te muevas	Dice que te calles y no te muevas
Direct Speech **Verb in Subjunctive**	**Indirect Speech** **Verb in Subjunctive**
¡Ojalá llueva! Si lloviese, no iríamos al zoo	Dice que ojalá llueva ...si lloviese no iríamos al zoo

When the main clause is in the Past Tense	
¿QUÉ DIJO/ HA DICHO/ HABÍA DICHO?	
Direct Speech **Verb in Indicative**	**Indirect Speech** **Verb in Indicative**
PRESENT- Como demasiado	PAST IMPERFECT- Comía demasiado
PAST IMPERFECT- Jugaba mucho a las cartas	PAST IMPERFECT- Jugaba mucho a las cartas
PAST INDEFINITE/ PERFECT- Fui/ había ido a Roma	PAST INDEFINITE/ PERFECT- Fue/ había ido a Roma
PRESENT PERFECT- He viajado poco	PAST PERFECT- Había viajado poco
FUTURE- Iré a Brasil	CONDITIONAL- Iría a Brasil
FUTURE PERFECT- Habré cantado más de ocho canciones	COMPOUND CONDITIONAL - Habría cantado más de ocho canciones

SIMPLE CONDITIONAL- Iría a las dos COMPOUND CONDITIONAL- Habría venido antes	SIMPLE CONDITIONAL- Iría a las dos COMPOUND CONDITIONAL- Habría venido antes
Direct Speech **Verb in Imperative**	**Indirect Speech** **Verb in Past Subjunctive**
No comas tanto y para de hablar	Dijo que no comiera tanto y que parase de hablar
Direct Speech **Verb in Subjunctive**	**Indirect Speech** **Verb in Past Subjunctive or** **Simple Conditional**
PRESENT- ¡Ojalá llueva! Quizás lo sepa Luis PRESENT PERFECT- Espero que lo hayas hecho.	PAST- Ojalá lloviese Quizás lo supiera Luis PAST PERFECT SUBJUNCTIVE - Esperaba que lo hubiera hecho

Exercises

1. Put in Indirect Speech what Jaime tells his daughter:
   ¿Por qué has llegado tan tarde?
   ¿Dónde estabas?
   ¡Ve a estudiar ahora mismo!
   Mañana hablaré con tu profesora.
   ¡Espero que no suspendas el examen!
   Jaime le preguntó que ....y le dijo
   que ....
   Le deseó que ....

2. Put in indirect speech the conversation between these people:
   "A" preguntó a "B" .... y "B" le contestó .....

   Juan   : ¿A qué hora irás a clase de inglés mañana?
   Miguel   : A las 5

   Susana   : ¿Qué tal es el restaurante "Sancho"?
   Esteban   : Muy bueno, siempre hay mucha gente.

   Gonzalo   : ¿Vas todos los días a la piscina?
   Pepe   : No, a veces voy a la playa

3. Underline the correct form:
   a) Si no (lloviera, lloverá, llueve) tanto (fuésemos, iríamos, iremos) al campo a pasar el día.
   b) Siempre que me (ponía, pongo, puse) este vestido me lo (mancho, mancharé, mancharía).
   c) Mañana (saldré, saldría, salgo) de viaje si todo (va, fuese, irá) bien.
   d) Si (estudiases, estudias, estudiabas) más (sacabas, sacarías, sacaste) mejores notas.
   e) Si (hubieras llegado, llegarías, llegaste) antes, (hubieses visto, habrías visto, verías) pasar el desfile.

Unit 15
EXPRESSING OPINIONS AND EXCHANGING IDEAS

Hablar de música/Talking about music

P: ¿Qué te parece el nuevo disco recopilatorio de los Beatles para regalárselo a Juan?

A: Está muy bien porque están las canciones más famosas, lo habría comprado esta mañana si hubiera tenido dinero.

P: No te preocupes. Podemos volver esta tarde.

P: What do you think of the new Beatles collection as a gift for Juan?

A: It's very good because it has all the famous songs. I would have bought it this morning if I had had money.

P: Don't worry. We can go back in the evening.

Hablar de cine/ Talking about films

A: Temía que no te gustase, como me habías dicho que no te gustaban las películas policiacas.

P: Me ha encantado. Es que había leído que no era demasiado buena.

A: No te fíes de la crítica, sólo les gusta un tipo de cine.

P: Sí es verdad, me ha encantado cuando el chico le dice a la actriz morena que iba a denunciarle a la policía.

A: Sí, y también cuando le cuenta a su hermano que tenía las pruebas en casa.

A: I was afraid that you might not like it, as you had told me that you don't like detective films.

P: It was enchanting. I had read that it wasn't too good.

A: Don't trust the critics. They only like one kind of films.

P: Yes, that's true. I really liked it when the boy tells the dark actress that he was going to give her away to the police.
A: Yes, and also when he tells his brother that he had the proofs at home.

Hablar de ropa, moda / Talking about clothes and fashion

A: Si yo pesara 5 kilos menos me compraría esos pantalones.
P: Yo creo que estás muy delgada, si adelgazaras unos quilos estarías horrible.
A: Sí claro, lo digo de broma. Opino que la delgadez de las modelos es extrema.
P: Sí, deberían prohibir que las modelos anoréxicas saliesen en los desfiles.

A: If I weighed five kilos less, I'd buy those trousers.
P: I think you are very thin. If you lost more weight, you'd look horrible.
A: Yes, of course. I'm just joking. I think that the models are extremely thin.
P: Yes, they must ban anorexic models from participating in fashion shows.

Hablar de política / Talking about politics

P: Yo no pienso votar, primero porque no lo tengo claro, segundo porque todos los partidos me parecen iguales.
A: ¿Cómo puedes decir eso? Si toda la gente hiciera como tú, la democracia dejaría de existir.
P: Sí, pero hay gente que no piensa como yo, además, estoy totalmente en desacuerdo con el sistema democrático, es como la dictadura de los que gobiernan.
A: ¿Cómo puedes hablar de esa forma? Eres muy intolerante.
P: En cuanto uno es un poco radical, le llaman intolerante.
A: ¿Y qué alternativa propondrías tú?
P: No sé, habrá que inventar otra cosa. ¿Cómo te explicas que la mayoría de los políticos sean economistas y no hayan estudiado ciencias políticas o historia?
A: En mi opinión, la economía es lo más importante.

P: I don't think I'll vote. Firstly because I'm not clear and secondly, because all the parties are the same.

A: How can you say such a thing? If everybody said the same thing, there wouldn't be any democracy.

P: Yes. But there many people who don't think like me. Moreover, I'm totally against the democratic system, it is like the dictatorship of those in power.

A: How can you speak like this? You are very intolerant.

P: The moment one gets a bit radical, everybody calls him intolerant.

A: And what alternative do you propose?

P: I don't know. One has to invent something. How is that the majority of politicians are economists and have not studied political science or history?

A: In my opinion, economics is the most important.

Cómo expresar opiniones / Expressing opinions

When we are talking about a theme, a fact or something that somebody has said we can use *indicative or subjunctive*:

¿Qué opinas sobre + lo/eso de que + va/vaya a haber una tercera guerra mundial?

(No) estoy de acuerdo con/en + lo/eso de que + va/vaya a haber una tercera guerra mundial.

When we are talking about a decision that somebody has taken, a proposal or a future act we use *subjunctive*:

¿Qué opinas sobre + lo/eso de que + nos aumenten el sueldo?

(No) estoy de acuerdo con/en + lo/eso de que + aumenten el sueldo.

Pienso/ creo/afirmo/niego + que + indicative

No pienso/creo/afirmo/niego + que + subjunctive

With Supongamos que/ Imaginemos que/ Pongamos que + *Indicative or Subjunctive* may be used depending on the context.

Present or future action - More probable to less probable:

Present Indicative - Supongamos que vienen

Present Subjunctive - Supongamos que vengan

Past Subjunctive - Supongamos que vinieran

Past action - More probable to less probable:

Present Perfect Indicative - Supongamos que ya han venido

Present Perfect Subjunctive - Supongamos que hayan venido.
Past Perfect Subjunctive - Supongamos que hubieran venido.

A mí me parece bien/mal/un error, + que + Subjunctive
Vale/merece la pena + que + Subjunctive
Es normal/ natural/ lógico/ conveniente/ necesario/ importante/ +
que + Subjunctive.

When the subject is not specified these expressions are used with
Infinitive:

Vale la pena estudiar español.

When the subject of the action is specified these expressions are
used with verb in the Subjunctive:
Vale la pena que estudies (tú) español.

Cómo preguntar a alguien su opinión/Asking for somebody's opinion

¿(Usted/Tú) qué opina/s sobre ...?
¿Cómo ve/s (usted/tú) ...?

Cómo expresar (des)acuerdo/ Expressing (dis)agreement

Estoy (totalmente/completamente) de acuerdo con/en ...
No estoy (en absoluto) de acuerdo con/en ...
(Pues, yo) no lo veo así (en absoluto).
(Yo) estoy (completamente/absolutamente) en contra de ...

Expressions for specific purposes

To organise a speech

- en mi opinión, a mi modo de ver, a mi juicio, para mí
- por otro lado, por otra parte, es más
- no obstante, sin embargo, ahora bien
- de todos modos, con todo, aún así
- por el contrario, en cambio
- con respecto a, en cuanto a, en lo referente a
- en conclusión, en definitiva, en resumen, en una palabra, en suma
- es decir, o sea, dicho de otro modo

To express cause and consequence

- con este fin
- por consiguiente
- por esta causa
- para ello
- por eso
- por lo tanto
- en consecuencia
- de ahí que
- por ello
- con este objeto

To specify

- precisemos
- para ser preciso
- yo diría que
- de hecho ...
- por otra parte
- he precisado al máximo sobre ...
- para ser claro ...

To enumerate

- no sólo ... sino también
- e incluso ...
- y también añado...
- primero, segundo, tercero ...
- en primer, segundo, tercer lugar
- finalmente
- por último
- por fin
- y para ser completo
- esto no es todo/ esto es todo.

To conclude or summarise

- para resumir diré ...
- resumo en una palabra/en algunas palabras ...
- en esencia lo que quiero decir/lo que he dicho ...
- lo que hay que retener es ...
- en resumen ....
- en pocas palabras ...
- lo podemos esquematizar así ...
- para acotar me limitaré a ...

To exemplify

- a modo de ejemplo
- y así vemos que ...
- por ejemplo
- como ilustración de lo que he dicho puede servir...
- este es un buen ejemplo
- podemos poner un ejemplo

To repeat

- te he repetido que ...
- te lo he repetido cien veces
- todavía una vez más te diré que ...
- pero, ¿cuántas veces hay que decírtelo?

To ask somebody to repeat

- Vd. perdone ¿puede repetir lo que ha dicho? No lo he oído/he entendido bien
- ¿Qué?, ¿Cómo?, ¿Qué ha dicho?, ¿Ha dicho ...?
- ¿Podría decirlo más alto? (Desde aquí no se oye)
- Ha dicho ..., ¿no?/¿verdad?
- ¿Es exactamente ...?

To ask somebody whether they have understood

No sé si queda/ha quedado claro que ...

To ask for clarifications or clarify

- No sé si te/le he entendido bien...
- No endiendo/he entendido bien lo que quiere/s decir...
- Tal vez/Quizás/ A lo mejor me he explicado mal, lo que quería decir ...

To interrupt to make a point

Perdon/un momento sólo quería aclarar (decir, añadir, explicar, etc.) que ....

To express certainity

Seguro que ...
Estoy seguro/a que...

To express ignorance

No lo sé
Ni idea

On getting to know something unexpected

¿Ah sí? No lo sabía

On realising that one was badly informed

Yo creía que...

To express worry

No sé qué tal me irá
No sé cómo saldrá
No sé si voy a encontrar trabajo...

To express resignation

¡Qué le vamos a hacer!
Así es la vida.

To express surprise or dismay

¡Qué curioso!
¡Qué raro!
Nunca + Present/ Past Perfect Indicative or Subjunctive + así
¡Nunca había visto nada igual!/ ¡Nunca hubiera dicho una cosa así!

To express satisfaction

¡Qué bien!
¡Qué bueno!
¡Qué buena idea!

To express sadness and share it

¡Qué pena!
¡Es una lástima!

To offer condolence

Lo siento mucho
Te/Le acompaño en el sentimiento

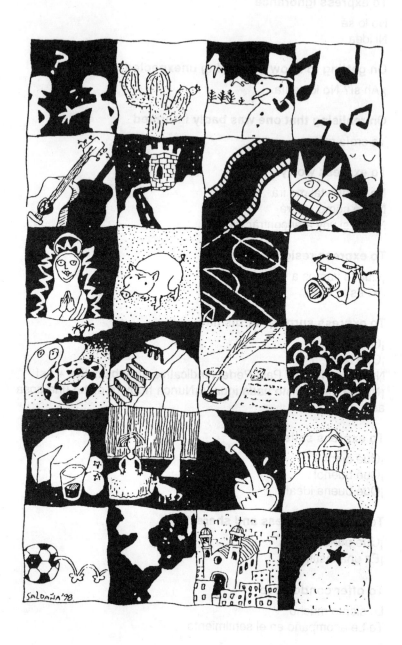

SALDAÑA '98

132

GRAMMAR

Conditional sentences

- Si + Past Subjunctive, + conditional is used when the condition is unlikely to be fulfilled or to express an unrealisable desire

Example:
Si hiciera sol, iríamos a la playa.

- Si + Past Perfect Subjuctive, + Compound Conditional is used to refer to unfulfilled conditions in the past, those which could have been fulfilled

Example:
Si ayer hubieras venido a mi casa, te habría devuelto el libro.

- **Me gustaría + Past Subjunctive**

When the subject is different in the two clauses, the Past subjunctive is used with *me gustaría*

Example:
Me gustaría que fueras a ver a tu abuela.

Exercises

1. Complete using Indicative or Subjunctive:
a) Manuel, perdona que no te (LLAMAR) .... el miércoles, es que tengo el teléfono estropeado.
b) En cuanto (ACABAR) .... esta novela, voy a empezar a escribir otra.
c) Anoche, cuando llegué a casa, mi hermana ya (IRSE) .... y no pude darle tu recado.
d) Quizás nos (COMPRAR, nosotros) .... una casa en la playa.
e) Mientras (ESTAR, yo) .... cocinando, (LLEGAR) .... Pedro de Suiza.
f) El sábado (PERDER, él) .... el reloj que le (REGALAR, yo) .... el viernes por la noche.

2. Join the two sentences as in the example:
Juan se ha comprado un coche. Es normal porque gana mucho dinero.

133

Es normal que Juan se haya comprado un coche porque gana mucho dinero.

a) Elisa no habla hindi a pesar de que hace 15 años que vive en Nueva Delhi. Es raro.
b) Todos esperaban el resultado de los análisis. Es normal, estaban preocupados.
c) Tuvo que pagar muchos impuestos. Es lógico, gana mucho dinero.
d) Han construído este edificio en dos meses. Es increíble.
e) Se ha cortado el pelo de nuevo. Es extraño, no le favorece nada.

3. Complete with Subjunctive:

a) Mientras (ESTAR) .... Juan trabajando aquí no nos cambiaremos de casa.
b) En cuanto (ACABAR, nosotras) .... la universidad, iremos de viaje.
c) A lo mejor voy a Estados Unidos y puede que (trabajar, yo) .... en la empresa de los González.
c) Si vosotros (IR) .... a la televisión, ganaríais ese concurso tan famoso.
d) Es probable que a Ramón lo (TRASLADAR) .... a otra ciudad.
e) Es preciso que (TERMINAR, vosotros) .... este trabajo antes del lunes.
f) Antes de que (SER) .... demasiado tarde, te diré lo que pienso de tu novio.

4. Translate the following sentences into Spanish:

a) I hope that the train reaches soon.
b) It is not necessary for Maria to come to the party.
c) It is incredible that Miguel earns so much money.
d) Even if it is cold we will go for a walk.
e) I have bought you this book so that you study.
f) I wish it rain soon.

APPENDIX 1

Nouns

All nouns in Spanish are masculine or feminine. Animate nouns have both forms – masculine and feminine. The easiest way to remember the gender is to learn the noun along with the article (*el* for masculine singular and *la* for feminine singular).

Some general gender classifications based on word endings:
- Most nouns ending in *-o, -or, -aje,* are masculine.

Examples:
  el perro, el libro, el coraje,

- Nouns ending in *-ista, -ma, -ta* are masculine like **el sistema, el taxista, el planeta.** When they refer to professions they have the same form for both masculine and feminine but are identified by the corresponding article.

Examples:
el artista/ la artista

- Most nouns ending in *-a,-dad, -tad, -ción, -sión, -zón, -ez, -tud, -dumbre* are feminine.

Examples:
  la estrella, la felicidad, la nación, la razón, la vejez, la multitud, la muchedumbre.

Gender Classifications according to meaning:
- Animate nouns referring to the masculine sex are masculine and those referring to the feminine sex are feminine. Sometimes the word is the same and the article differentiates the gender. In other cases, the endings change from *–o* to *–a.* In some other cases, different words are used.

Examples:
el hombre/ la mujer
el abuelo/ la abuela
el perro/ la perra
el artista / la artista

* The names of the days of the week and months are masculine.
Examples:
el lunes, enero, etc.

* The names of rivers, oceans, seas and mountain ranges are masculine.
Examples:
el Pacífico, el Yamuna, los Himalayas, etc

* Professions traditionally exercised by men are used in the masculine form, even when they refer to women; very often, the masculine form is used with the feminine article.
Examples:
el médico/ la médico
el arquitecto/ la arquitecto

* The names of the letters of the alphabet are feminine.
Examples:
la eñe, la efe.

* Most of the fruits are feminine and the fruit-bearing trees are masculine.
Examples:
la manzana – el manzano
la naranja – el naranjo

Masculine and Feminine Suffixes:
* The feminine form is obtained by adding **-a** to the masculine forms ending in **–o, -or, -l**.
Examples:
el doctor/ la doctora
el chico/ la chica
el chaval/ la chavala

- **-esa, -isa, -triz** are feminine suffixes.

Examples:

el actor/ la actriz

el poeta/ la poetisa

el príncipe/ la princesa

- Nouns ending in **–ista** and **–nte** (not all) refer to both genders.

Examples:

el estudiante/ la estudiante

el periodista/ la periodista

el cantante/ la cantante

Note: Throughout the book, the vocabulary is introduced with the corresponding articles in order to facilitate learning.

Noun plurals

- If a noun ends in a vowel, it takes **-s** in the plural form and if it ends in a consonant it takes **–es.**

Examples:

la casa/ las casas

el árbol/ los árboles

- Nouns that end in **–z** take **–ces** in the plural form.

Example:

la luz/ las luces

- Nouns that end with a stressed **–í** take **–es** in the plural.

Example:

rubí/ rubíes

APPENDIX 2

Regular Verbs

We give below the conjugation pattern of three regular verbs in all the tenses used in Spanish. They are hablar, comer and vivir.

Hablar
Indicative

Present	Past Imperfect	Past Indefinite	Future	Conditional
hablo	hablaba	hablé	hablaré	hablaría
hablas	hablabas	hablaste	hablarás	hablarías
habla	hablaba	habló	hablará	hablaría
hablamos	hablábamos	hablamos	hablaremos	hablaríamos
habláis	hablabais	hablasteis	hablaréis	hablaríais
hablan	hablaban	hablaron	hablarán	hablarían

Present Perfect	Past Perfect	Future Perfect	Compound Conditional
he hablado	había hablado	habré hablado	habría hablado
has hablado	habías hablado	habrás hablado	habrías hablado
ha hablado	había hablado	habrá hablado	habría hablado
hemos hablado	habíamos hablado	habremos hablado	habríamos hablado
habéis hablado	habíais hablado	habréis hablado	habríais hablado
han hablado	habían hablado	habrán hablado	habrían hablado

Subjuntive

Present	Past	Present Perfect	Past Perfect
hable	hablara	haya hablado	hubiera hablado
hables	hablaras	hayas hablado	hubieras hablado
hable	hablara	haya hablado	hubiera hablado
hablemos	habláramos	hayamos hablado	hubiéramos hablado
habléis	hablarais	hayáis hablado	hubierais hablado
hablen	hablaran	hayan hablado	hubieran hablado

Imperative

habla /	no hables
hable /	no hables
hablad /	no habléis
hablen /	no hablen

Impersonal Forms

Infinitive	:	hablar
Participle	:	hablado
Gerund	:	hablando

Comer

Indicative

Present	Past Imperfect	Past Indefinite	Future	Conditional
como	comía	comí	comeré	comería
comes	comías	comiste	comerás	comerías
come	comía	comió	comerá	comería
comemos	comíamos	comimos	comeremos	comeríamos
coméis	comíais	comisteis	comeréis	comeríais
comen	comían	comieron	comerán	comerían

Present Perfect	Past Perfect	Future Perfect	Compound Conditional
he comido	había comido	habré comido	habría comido
has comido	habías comido	habrás comido	habrías comido
ha comido	había comido	habrá comido	habría comido
hemos comido	habíamos comido	habremos comido	habríamos comido
habéis comido	habíais comido	habréis comido	habríais comido
han comido	habían comido	habrán comido	habrían comido

Subjuntive

Present	Past	Present Perfect	Past Perfect
coma	comiera	haya comido	hubiera comido
comas	comieras	hayas comido	hubieras comido
coma	comiera	haya comido	hubiera comido
comamos	comiéramos	hayamos comido	hubiéramos comido
comáis	comierais	hayáis comido	hubierais comido
coman	comieran	hayan comido	hubieran comido

Imperative

come / no comas
coma / no coma
comed / no comáis
coman / no coman

Impersonal Forms

Infinitive : comer
Participle : comido
Gerund   : comiendo

Vivir

Indicative

Present	Past Imperfect	Past Indefinite	Future	Conditional
vivo	vivía	viví	viviré	viviría
vives	vivías	viviste ◄	vivirás	vivirías
vive	vivía	vivió	vivirá	viviría
vivimos	vivíamos	vivimos	viviremos	viviríamos
vivís	vivíais	vivisteis	viviréis	viviríais
viven	vivían	vivieron	vivirán	vivirían

Present Perfect	Past Perfect	Future Perfect	Compound Conditional
he vivido	había vivido	habré vivido	habría vivido
has vivido	habías vivido	habrás vivido	habrías vivido
ha vivido	había vivido	habrá vivido	habría vivido
hemos vivido	habíamos vivido	habremos vivido	habríamos vivido
habéis vivido	habíais vivido	habréis vivido	habríais vivido
han vivido	habían vivido	habrán vivido	habrían vivido

Subjuntive

Present	Past	Present Perfect	Past Perfect
viva	viviera	haya vivido	hubiera vivido
vivas	vivieras	hayas vivido	hubieras vivido
viva	viviera	haya vivido	hubiera vivido
vivamos	viviéramos	hayamos vivido	hubiéramos vivido
viváis	vivierais	hayáis vivido	hubierais vivido
vivan	vivieran	hayan vivido	hubieran vivido

Imperative

vive/ no vivas
viva / no viva
vivid / no viváis
vivan / no vivan

Impersonal Forms

Infinitive : vivir
Participle : vivido
Gerund : viviendo

140

Irregular Verbs

We have given the irregular patterns in the conjugation of different tenses.

1) Irregular Verbs in the Present Indicative, Present Subjunctive and Imperative.

1)	E, I>IE	Indicative	Subjuntive	Imperative
	Pensar	pienso	piense	
	Adquirir	piensas	pienses	piensa / piense
	Atravesar	piensa	piense	
	Despertar	pensamos	pensemos	
	Empezar	pensáis	penséis	pensad / piensen
	Recomendar	piensa	piensen	
	Merendar			
	Negar			
	Sentir			

2)	O,U>UE	Indicative	Subjuntive	Imperative
	Contar	cuento	cuente	
	Dormir	cuentas	cuentes	cuenta / cuente
	Acordar	cuenta	cuente	
	Recordar	contamos	contemos	
	Costar	contáis	contéis	contad / cuenten
	Mostrar	cuentan	cuenten	
	Jugar			
	Volar			
	Volver			

3)	N>NG	Indicative	Subjuntive	Imperative
	Poner	pongo	ponga	
	Tener	pones	pongas	pon / ponga
	Obtener	pone	ponga	
	Prevenir	ponemos	pongamos	
	Detener	ponéis	pongáis	poned / pongan
	Suponer	ponen	pongan	
	Mantener			

4)	C>G	Indicative	Subjuntive	Imperative
	Hacer	hago	haga	
	Deshacer	haces	hagas	haz / haga
	Satisfacer	hace	haga	
	Yacer	hacemos	hagamos	
		hacéis	hagáis	haced / hagan
		hacen	hagan	

5)	E>I	Indicative	Subjuntive	Imperative
	Pedir	pido	pida	
	Despedir	pides	pidas	pide / pida
	Vestir	pide	pida	
	Seguir	pedimos	pidamos	
	Corregir	pedís	pidáis	pedid / pidan
	Servir	piden	pidan	
6)	C>ZC	Indicative	Subjuntive	Imperative
	Conocer	conozco	conozca	
	Parecer	conoces	conozcas	conoce / conozca
	Conducir	conoce	conozca	
	Lucir	conocemos	conozcamos	
	Traducir	conocéis	conozcáis	conoced / conozcan
	Nacer	conocen	conozcan	
	Introducir			

7)	Verbs which are only irregular in the Imperative tú form:			
	Salir	Sal	Tener	Ten
	Hacer	Haz	Ir	Ve
	Poner	Pon	Decir	Di
	Venir	Ven	Ser	Sé

2) Irregular Verbs in the Future and Conditional

	Future	Conditional
Saber	sabré	sabría
Poner	pondré	pondría
Querer	querré	querría
Hacer	haré	haría
Decir	diré	diría
Salir	saldré	saldría
Poder	podré	podría
Venir	vendré	vendría
Tener	tendré	tendría

3) Irregular Verbs in the Past Indefinite and Past Subjunctive

	Past Indefinite	Past Subjuntive
Traer	traje	trajera
Decir	dije	dijera
Hacer	hice	hiciera
Querer	quise	quisiera
Venir	vine	viniera
Saber	supe	supiera
Andar	anduve	anduviera

Conducir	conduje	condujera
Estar	estuve	estuviera
Caber	cupe	cupiera
Poner	puse	pusiera
Poder	pude	pudiera
Tener	tuve	tuviera
Ver	vi	viera
Ser	fui	fuera
Ir	fui	fuera
Dar	di	diera

Note : Only the first person singular form is given in the above lists.

4) Irregular Participles

	Participle
Decir	dicho
Hacer	hecho
Abrir	abierto
Absolver	absuelto
Cubrir	cubierto
Descubrir	descubierto
Describir	descrito
Devolver	devuelto
Disponer	dispuesto
Envolver	envuelto
Escribir	escrito
Disolver	disuelto
Freir	frito
Volver	vuelto
Poner	puesto

SER

Indicative

Present	Past Imperfect	Past Indefinite	Future	Conditional
soy	era	fui	seré	sería
eres	eras	fuiste	serás	serías
es	era	fue	será	sería
somos	éramos	fuimos	seremos	seríamos
sois	erais	fuisteis	seréis	seríais
son	eran	fueron	serán	serían

143

Present Perfect	Past Perfect	Future Perfect	Compound Conditional
he sido	había sido	habré sido	habría sido
has sido	habías sido	habrás sido	habrías sido
ha sido	había sido	habrá sido	habría sido
hemos sido	habíamos sido	habremos sido	habríamos sido
habéis sido	habíais sido	habréis sido	habríais sido
han sido	habían sido	habrán sido	habrían sido

Subjuntive

Present	Past	Present Perfect	Past Perfect
sea	fuera/ fuese	haya sido	hubiera/ hubiese sido
seas	fueras/ fueses	hayas sido	hubieras/ hubieses sido
sea	fuera/ fuese	haya sido	hubiera/ hubiese sido
seamos	fuéramos/ fuésemos	hayamos sido	hubiéramos/ hubiésemos sido
seáis	fuerais/ fueseis	hayáis sido	hubierais / hubieseis sido
sean	fueran/ fuesen	hayan sido	hubieran/ hubiesen sido

Imperative

se/   no seas
sea/   no sea
sed/   no seáis
sean/ no sean

Impersonal Forms

Infinitive : ser
Participle : sido
Gerund   : siendo

IR
Indicative

Present	Past Imperfect	Past Indefinite	Future	Conditional
voy	iba	fui	iré	iría
vas	ibas	fuiste	irás	irías
va	iba	fue	irá	iría
vamos	íbamos	fuimos	iremos	iríamos
vais	ibais	fuisteis	ireréis	iríais
van	iban	fueron	irán	irían

Present Perfect	Past Perfect	Future Perfect	Compound Conditional
he ido	había ido	habré ido	habría ido
has ido	habías ido	habrás ido	habrías ido
ha ido	había ido	habrá ido	habría ido
hemos ido	habíamos ido	habremos ido	habríamos ido
habéis ido	habíais ido	habréis ido	habríais ido
han ido	habían ido	habrán ido	habrían ido

Subjunctive

Present	Past	Present Perfect	Past Perfect
vaya	fuera/ fuese	haya ido	hubiera/ hubiese ido
vayas	fueras/ fueses	hayas ido	hubieras/ hubieses ido
vaya	fuera/ fuese	haya ido	hubiera/ hubiese ido
vayamos	fuéramos/ fuésemos	hayamos ido	hubiéramos/ hubiésemos ido
vayáis	fuerais/ fueseis	hayáis ido	hubierais / hubieseis ido
vayan	fueran/ fuesen	hayan ido	hubieran/ hubiesen ido

Imperative

ve/	no vayas
vaya/	no vaya
id/	no vayáis
vayan/	no vayan

Impersonal Forms

Infinitive : ir
Participle : ido
Gerund : yendo

LIST OF VERBS

(Spanish to English)

abrir	to open	bailar	to dance
aburrirse	to get bored	bajar	to get down
acabar	to finish	bañarse	to bathe
acompañar	to accompany	beber	to drink
aconsejar	to advise	buscar	to look for
acordarse	to remember		
acostarse	to go to bed	calentar	to heat up
adelgazar	to lose weight	callarse	to shut up
adquirir	to acquire	cambiar	to change
afeitarse	to shave	caminar	to walk
afirmar	to affirm	cancelar	to cancel
agradecer	to thank	casarse	to marry
ahorrar	to save	cenar	to have dinner
almorzar	to have lunch	cerrar	to close
alquilar	to rent	charlar	to chat
andar	to walk	cobrar	to charge /
añadir	to add		to recover
apagar la	to turn off the	cocinar	to cook
televisión	television	coger	to catch
aparcar	to park	comer	to eat
aparecer	to appear	compartir	to share
apetecer	to feel like,	comprar	to buy
	to wish	comprender	to understand
apreciar	to appreciate	confiar	to confide
aprender	to learn	confirmar	to confirm
aprobar	to pass (an exam)	conocer	to know (a person or
asar	to roast		a place)
asistir	to attend (a class)	conseguir	to get
atender	to attend	consultar	to consult
atravesar	to pass through	contar	to count / to narrate
atreverse	to dare	contestar	to answer
ayudar	to help	conversar	to converse

146

corregir	to correct	empatar	to equalize
correr	to run	empezar	to begin
cortar	to cut	encender la	to turn on the
costar	to cost	televisión	television
creer	to think / to believe	encontrar	to find
cruzar	to cross	encontrarse	to meet
cubrir	to cover	enfriar	to become cold
		enseñar	to teach/to show
dar	to give	entender	to understand
dar la mano	to shake hands	entrar	to enter
darse cuenta de	to realise	entrevistar	to interview
deber	to have to	enviar	to send
decidir	to decide	escribir	to write
decir	to tell / to say	escuchar	to listen
dedicarse	to have a job	esperar	to wait/to hope
dejar	to leave/ to let	esquiar	to ski
deletrear	to spell out	estar	to be
denunciar	to lodge a complaint /	estar acostado	to be lying down
	to report	estar andando	to be walking
depender	to depend	estar de pie	to be standing (up)
desayunar	to have breakfast	estar de	to be on vacations
descansar	to rest	vacaciones	
describir	to describe	estar embara-	to be pregnant
descubrir	to discover	zada/ estar	
desear	to want	en estado	
desnudarse/	to undress	estar en forma	to be fit
desvestirse		estar moviéndose	to be moving
despedirse	to say goodbye/ to	estar sentado	to be seated
	take leave	estudiar	to study
despertarse	to wake up	evitar	to avoid
detener	to detain	existir	to exist
devolver	to return (a thing)	explicar	to explain
disfrutar	to enjoy		
divertirse	to enjoy/ to amuse	fiarse	to trust
	oneself	firmar	to sign
doler	to pain	freir	to fry
dormir	to sleep	fumar	to smoke
ducharse	to have a shower	funcionar	to function
dudar	to doubt		
		ganar	to win
echar	to throw/to put in	girar	to turn
echar al correo	to post (a letter)	gobernar	to rule
embarcar	to embark	granizar	to hail

guardar	to keep	merecer	to deserve
gustar	to like	merendar	to have tea
		meter	to put in
haber (hay)		mirar	to look/ to have a look
hablar	to speak		
hacer	to do	molestar(se)	to bother/ to disturb
hacer cola	to make a queue		
hacerse	to become	morir	to die
hervir	to boil	mostrar	to show
		moverse	to move
imaginar	to imagine		
importar(le) algo a alguien	to matter (something to somebody)	nacer	to be born
		nadar	to swim
		navegar	to sail
incluir	in include	necesitar	to need
ingresar dinero	to deposit money	negar	to deny, to refuse
intentar	to try	nevar	to snow
interesarse por/en	to be interested about/in		
		obtener	to obtain
invertir	to invest	ocurrir	to occur
invitar	to invite	ofrecer	to offer
ir	to go	oír	to hear
		oler	to smell
jugar	to play	olvidarse	to forget
		opinar	to have an opinion
lavar	to clean		
lavarse	to wash oneself	pagar	to pay
leer	to read	parar	to stop
levantarse	to get up	parecer	to seem
llamar	to call	parecerse	to resemble
llamarse	to call oneself	pasar	to pass
llegar	to arrive/to reach	pasar las vacaciones	to spend the vacations
llegar a tener	to obtain		
llenar	to fill	pasárselo bien/mal	to have a good time
llevar	to take/ to wear		
llorar	to cry	pasear	to take to walk
llover	to rain	peinarse	to comb one's hair
luchar	to fight	pelar	to peel
		pensar	to think
mandar	to send/ to order	perder	to lose
marcar	to mark/ to dial	perdonar	to excuse
marcharse	to go away	pertenecer	to belong
mejorarse	to get better	pesar	to weigh

pescar	to fish	reirse	to laugh
picar (algo)	to have a bite/ to chop	rellenar	to fill up
		repetir	to repeat
pintar	to paint	reservar	to reserve
planchar	to iron	retirarse	to remove oneself
poder	to be able to	retrasar	to delay/ to postpone
poner	to put		
poner una multa	to fine	robar	to steal
		rodear	to surround
ponerse	to put on	rogar	to request
preferir	to prefer		
preguntar por	to ask about/ to enquire	saber	to know
		sacar	to take out
preocuparse	to worry	sacar dinero	to withdraw
preparar	to prepare	salir	to leave (from)/ to go out
presentar	to introduce		
probar	to taste / to prove	satisfacer	to satisfy
probarse	to try on	seguir	to follow/ to continue
prohibir	to disallow/ to prohibit		
		sentarse	to sit down
prometer	to promise	sentir	to feel .
proponer	to propose	ser	to be
		servir	to serve
quedar	to suit/ to remain	soportar	to tolerate
quedar bien/ mal	to suit	sorprenderse	to be surprised
		sugerir	to suggest
quedar con	to make an appointment with somebody	suponer	to suppose
		suspender	to fail
quedar en	to agree on/to	tapar	to cover
quedarse	to stay/ to remain	tardar	to be late/to take a long time
quedarse (con) algo	to keep something		
querer	to want	temer	to fear
quitar (se)	to remove/to take off	tener	to have
		tener calor	to be hot
reaccionar	to react	tener frío	to be cold
recibir	to receive	tener ganas de	to desire
recoger	to collect	tener hambre	to be hungry
recoger a alguien	to pick someone up	tener la culpa	to be at fault
		tener prisa	to be in a hurry
recomendar	to recommend	tener razón	to be right
recordar	to remember	tener sed	to be thirsty
regalar	to gift		

tener sueño	to be sleepy	traducir	to translate
terminar	to finish	traer	to bring
tocar	to touch	tratar	to treat/ to try
tocar la lotería	to win a lottery		
tocar un instrumento	to play an instrument	unirse	to join
tomar	to take	valer	to be worth
tomar copas	to have a drink	venir	to come
tomar el aperitivo	to have an aperitif	ver	to see
		viajar	to travel
tomar el sol	to sunbathe	visitar	to visit
torcer	to turn	vivir	to live
tostar	to toast	volver	to return from/ to come back
trabajar	to work		
trabajar la tierra	to till the land	votar	to vote

VOCABULARY

(Spanish to English)

A

abajo	down	albañil	mason
abogado/a	lawyer	albergue (el)	youth hostel
abrigo (el)	coat	aldea (la)	hamlet
abrir	to open	alemán / a	German
abuelo/a	grandfather/	alfombra (la)	carpet
	grandmother	algo	something
aburrido/a	boring	algodón (el)	cotton
acción (la)	shares / action	alguien	someone
aceite (el)	oil	allí	there
aceituna (la)	olive	almohada (la)	pillow
acelerador (el)	accelerator	almorzar	to have lunch
acera (la)	pavement	almuerzo (el)	midday meal
acomodador(el)	usher	alquilar	to rent
acompañar	to accompany	altavoz (el)	(loud) speaker
acostarse	to go to bed	alto/a	tall
actor (el)	actor	alubias (las)	kidney bean
actriz (la)	actress	alumno/a	student / pupil
aduana (la)	customs	amable	kind / polite
adulto/a	adult	ama/o de casa	housewife / house
aeropuerto (el)	airport		husband
afeitarse	to shave	amargo / a	bitter
agencia de	travel agency	amarillo / a	yellow
viajes (la)		ambulancia (el)	ambulance
agradable	pleasant	americano / a	American
agradecer	to thank	amigo/a	friend
agricultor/a	farmer	ancho/a	wide/ broad
agrio (el)	sour	anciano/a	old man/woman
agua (el)	water	andén (el)	platform
ahorrar	to save	anfitrión/a	host / hostess
aire (el)	air	anillo (el)	ring
ajo (el)	garlic	antena (la)	antenna

151

antiguo/a	old
antipático/a	unkind
anuncio (el)	advertisement
año (el)	year
apagar la televisión	to turn off the television
aparcamiento(el)	parking
apartamento (el)	apartment
apellido (el)	surname
aprender	to learn
aprobar	to pass (an exam)
aquí	here
árbitro (el)	referee
árbol (el)	tree
arcén (el)	border (of the road)
arena (la)	sand
argentino / a	Argentinean
armario (el)	cupboard/ wardrobe
arquitecto / a	architect
arriba	up
artículo (el)	article
artista (el / la)	artist
ascensor (el)	lift / elevator
aseo (el)	toilet
asiento (el)	seat
asignatura (la)	subject / paper
atender	to attend to
atletismo (el)	athletics
atún (el)	tuna fish
autobús (el)	bus
autopista (la)	motorway/ highway
avión (el)	plane
ayer	yesterday
ayudar	to help
azafata / o	air hostess / steward
azúcar (el)	sugar
azul	blue

B

bailar	to dance
bajar	to get down
bajo	short
balcón (el)	balcony
balón (el)/ pelota	(la) ball
baloncesto (el)	basketball
banco (el)	bank/ bench
bañarse	to bathe
bañera (la)	bathtub
barato/a	cheap
barba (la)	beard
barco (el)	ship
barrio (el)	colony/ neighbourhood
bastante	enough/quite
batería (la)	drums / battery
batidora (la)	food mixer
berenjena (la)	aubergine/ brinjal
bicicleta (la)	bicycle
bienvenido/a	welcome
billete (el)	ticket
blanco/a	white
blusa (la)	blouse
boca (la)	mouth
bocadillo (el)	sandwich
boliviano/a	Bolivian
bolsa (la)	stock market/ plastic or cloth carry bag
bolsa de viaje (la)	travel bag
bolso (el)	bag/ handbag
bonito/a	beautiful
bosque (el)	woods
bote (el)	can
botella (la)	bottle
brasileño/a	Brazilian
brazo (el)	arm
bueno/bien	well/ actually
bueno/a	good
burro /a	donkey

buscar	to look for
butaca (la)	seat

C

caballo (el)	horse
cabeza (la)	head
cabina (la)	cabin
cabina de teléfonos (la)	telephone booth
cabo (el)	cape
cacerola (la)	casserole / saucepan
café (el)	coffee
caja (la)	box/ cash counter
cajafuerte (la)	safe
cajero /a	cashier
cajero autómatico(el)	automatic teller machine
calabaza (la)	pumpkin
calcetines (los)	socks
caldo (el)	broth/ clear soup
calentar	to heat
caliente	hot
calle (la)	street
cama (la)	bed
camarero/a	waiter/waitress
cambiar	to change
camilla (la)	stretcher
camión (el)	truck
camionero / a	truck driver
camiseta (la)	t -shirt
campo (el)	country side
campo de fútbol (el)	pitch/soccer field
cancelar	to cancel
cancha (la)/ pista (la)	court
cansado/a	tired
cantante (el/ la)	singer
característica (la)	characteristic
carne (la)	meat
carnicería (la)	meat shop
caro/a	expensive
carpintero / a	carpenter
carretera (la)	road
carril (el)	track/ lane
carro (el)	cart
carta (la)	letter/ menu
cartelera (la)	billboard
cartera (la)	wallet
cartero / a	postman
casado/a	married
casi nunca	almost never
casi siempre	almost always
castillo (el)	castle
casualidad (la)	chance
catedral (la)	cathedral
catedrático / a	professor
cebolla (la)	onion
celoso/a	jealous
cena (la)	dinner
cenar	to have dinner
centro (el)	centre
cepillo (el)	brush
cepillo de dientes (el)	toothbrush
cerca	near
cerdo (el)	pig/pork
cereza (la)	cherry
cerilla (la)	match-stick
cerrar	to close
cerveza (la)	beer
champú (el)	shampoo
chaqueta (la)	jacket
charlar	to chat
chileno / a	Chilean
chino / a	Chinese
chofér	chauffeur / driver
chorizo (el)	hard pork sausage/salami
científico / a	scientist
cine (el)	cinema
cinturón (el)	belt
ciudad (la)	town
claro/a	light, clear
clase (la)	class

clásico/a	classic	contento/a	happy
clínica (la)	clinic	contestar	to answer
coche (el)	car	control de	passport control
coche cama (el)	sleeping wagon	pasaportes (el)	
cocido/a	cooked	conversar	to talk / to
cocina (la)	kitchen		converse
cocinar	to cook	copa (la)	glass / cup
cocinero / a	cook	corazón (el)	heart
codo (el)	elbow	corbata (la)	tie
coger	to catch	cordero (el)	lamb/ mutton
col (la)	cabbage	cordillera (la)	mountain range
cola (la)	queue	correos	post office
colchón (el)	mattress	correr	to run
coliflor (la)	cauliflower	corrida (la)	bullfight
colina (la)	hill	cortar	to cut
collar (el)	necklace	cortina (la)	curtain
colombiano / a	Colombian	corto/a	short
comedor (el)	dining room	cosa (la)	thing
comer	to eat	costa (la)	coast
comida (la)	lunch	crudo/a	raw
cómodo/a	comfortable	cruzar	to cross
compañero/a	colleague	cuaderno (el)	notebook
compañero/a	flatmate	cuadrado/a	square
de piso		cuadro (el)	painting
compartir	to share	cuarto de baño (el)	bathroom
comprar	to buy	cubano / a	Cuban
compras (las)	shopping	cubierta (la)	deck
comprender	to understand	cubiertos (los)	cutlery
comunista (el/la)	communist	cuchara (la)	spoon
concierto (el)	concert	cuchillo (el)	knife
conductor / a	driver	cuello (el)	neck
confirmar	to confirm	cuenco (el)	bowl
conocer	to know	cuenta (la)	bill
consejo de	council of	cuenta	current account
ministros (el)	ministers	corriente (la)	
conservador / a	conservative	cuenta de	savings
consigna (la)	left-luggage office	ahorro (la)	account
consulta (la)	consulting	cuero (el)	leather
	chamber	cuñado/a	brother/sister in
consultar	to consult		law
contar	to count/ to narrate	curso (el)	course

D

dar	to give
dar la mano	to shake hands
darse cuenta (de)	to realise
dársena (la)	dock
deber	to have to/ duty
débil	weak
decidir	to decide
decir	to say / to tell
decorado/a	scenary
decorador / a	interior decorator
dedicarse	to have a job
dedo (el)	finger
dejar de	to give up something
delante de	in front of
deletrear	to spell out
delgado/a	thin
demasiado	too much
depender	to depend
dependiente (el / la)	shop assistant
deporte (el)	sport
deportista (el / la)	sportsman
deportivo / a	sporty
derecha	right
desagradable	unpleasant
desayunar	to have breakfast
desayuno (el)	breakfast
descansar	to rest
describir	to describe
descuento (el)	discount
desear	to want/ to desire
desnudarse/ desvestirse	to get undressed
después de	after
destino (el)	destination/ destiny
detergente (el)	detergent/ washing powder
detrás de	behind
día (el)	day

día festivo (el)	holiday
diccionario (el)	dictionary
difícil	difficult
dinero (el)	cash/ money
diploma (el)	diploma
diplomado/a	graduate
diputado (el)/ senador (el)	senator/ minister
dirección (la)	address
director/a	manager, principal
discoteca (la)	discothèque
diseñador/a	designer
divertido/a	funny
divertirse	to enjoy, to amuse oneself
divorciado/a	divorced
doctor/a	doctor
doctorado/a	PhD
dolor (el)	pain
domingo (el)	Sunday
dormitorio (el)	bedroom
droguería (la)	store where cleaning materials are sold
ducha (la)	shower
dulce	sweet

E

edad (la)	age
edificio (el)	building
educación (la)	education
elecciones (las)	elections
electricista (el / la)	electrician
elegante	elegant
embarcar	to embark
embutido (el)	sausage
empatar	to equalize/ to draw/ to tie
empezar	to begin/ to start
empleado/a	employee

empresa (la)	company	estación de)	railway station
empresario/a	manager	trenes (la	
en	in	estación del	season of the
encender	to turn on the	año (la)	year
la televisión	television	estado civil (el)	civil status
enchufe (el)	plug	estampado/a	printed (material
encima	above		or cloth)
encontrar	to find	estanco (el)	tobacco shop /
encontrarse	to meet		stand
enfermero/a	nurse	estantería (la)	shelf
enfermo/a	ill/ sick	estar	to be
enfrente (de)	in front (of)	estar acostado	to be in bed
enfriar	to become cold	estar alegre	to be happy
ensalada (la)	salad	estar andando	to be walking
enseñanza (la)	education	estar contento	to be glad
enseñar	to teach/ to show	estar de pie	to be standing
entonces	then		(up)
entrar	to enter	estar embarazada	to be
entrevistar	to interview	/estar en estado	pregnant
enviar	to send	estar moviéndose	to be moving
envidioso/a	envious	estar sentado	to be sitting
equipaje (el)	luggage		down
equipo (el)	team	estar triste	to be sad
escala (la)	scale	este	east/ this
escaleras (las)	stairs	estómago (el)	stomach
escaparate (el)	shop window	estrecho/a	narrow
escayola (la)	plaster	estudiante (el / la)	student
escribir	to write	estudiar	to study
escritor / a	writer	estupendo/a	great
escuchar	to listen	examen (el)	exam
escuela (la)/	school	explicar	to explain
colegio (el)		extranjero/a	foreign/ abroad
espalda (la)	back	extraño/a	strange
español / a	Spanish		
espectador/a	spectator	**F**	
espejo (el)	mirror	fábrica (la)	factory
esperar	to wait	fácil	easy
espinacas (las)	spinach	facturación de	lugagge
esponja (la)	sponge	equipajes (la)	registration
esquiar	to ski	falda (la)	skirt
esquina (la)	corner	familia (la)	family
estación de	bus terminal	farmacia (la)	chemist shop
autobuses (la)		farola (la)	lamppost

fecha (la)	date	gato/a	cat
feliz	happy	gel (el)	gel
feo/a	ugly	generoso/a	generous
fiambrera (la)	lunchbox	gente (la)	people
fiesta (la)	party	gimnasia (la)	gymnastics
fila (la)	row/ line	golfo (el)	gulf
fin de semana (el)	week end	gordo/a	fat
final (el)	end	gracias (las)	thanks
firmar	to sign	grado (el)	degree
física (la)	Physics	grande	big
flaco/a	skinny	grandes	departmental
flor (la)	flower	almacenes (los)	stores
fontanero / o	plumber	granizar	to hail
foto (la)	photo	grifo (el)	tap
francés / a	French	gris	grey
fregadero (el)	sink	grosero/a	rude/ indecent
freir	to fry	grúa (la)	crane
freno (el)	brake	guantera (la)	glove
freno de mano (el)	handbrake		compartment
fresa (la)	strawberry	guapo/a	beautiful/
fresco/a	fresh		handsome/ pretty
fruta (la)	fruit	guatemalteco / a	Guatemalan
fuente (la)	serving dish/	guía	guide/city map
	fountain	guindilla (la)	chilli
fuerte	strong	guisante (el)	pea
función (la)	function/ show	guitarra (la)	guitar
funcionar	to function	gustar	to like
funcionario/a	government		
	employee	**H**	
fútbol (el)	football		
		habitación (la)	room
G		habitación doble (la)	double room
		habitación sencilla (la)	single room
gallina (la)	hen		
gallo (el)	cock	hablar	to speak
gamba (la)	prawn	hacer	to do
ganar	to win	hacerse	to become
garaje (el)	garage	harina (la)	flour
garbanzos (los)	chick peas	helado (el)	ice cream
garganta (la)	throat	herida	injury/ wound
gasóleo (el)	diesel oil	herido/a	injured (person)
gasolina (la)	petrol	hermano/a	brother/ sister
gasolinera (la)	petrol station		

hervir	to boil	invierno (el)	winter
hielo (el)	ice	inyección (la)	injection
hierba (la)	grass	ir	to go
higiene (la)	hygiene	isla (la)	island
hijo/a	son/ daughter	italiano / a	Italian
historia (la)	history/ story	izquierda	left
hoja (la)	leaf/sheet of paper		

J

hombre (el)	man		
hombro (el)	shoulder	jabón (el)	soap
hora (la)	time/ hour	jamón (el)	ham
horario (el)	timetable	japonés/a	Japanese
horno (el)	oven	jarabe (el)	syrup
horrible	horrible	jarra (la)	jug
hospital (el)	hospital	jersei (el)	sweater
hoy	today	joven	young
huelga (la)	strike	judías (las)	beans
huevo (el)	egg	judo (el)	judo
		jueves (el)	Thursday
		juez/a	umpire/ judge
		jugar	to play

I

ideal	ideal	justicia (la)	justice
idioma (el)	language		
iglesia (la)	church		

L

ilustración (la)	picture/ illustration	ladera (la)	slope
importancia (la)	importance	lago (el)	lake
incómodo/a	uncomfortable	lámpara (la)	lamp
indio / a	Indian	lana (la)	wool
industria (la)	industry	langosta (la)	lobster
informativo (el)	newscast	lápiz (el)	pencil
informe (el)	report	largo/a	long
infusión (la)	infusion	lata (la)	tin
ingeniero / a	engineer	lavadora (la)	washing machine
inglés / a	English		
ingresar dinero	to deposit money	lavandería (la)	laundry service
instituto (el)	institute	lavaplatos (el)	dishwasher
inteligente	intelligent	lavar	to clean
interesante	interesting	lavarse	to wash oneself
interesarse por/ en	to be interested about/in	leche (la)	milk
		lechuga (la)	lettuce
intermitente (el)	blinker	leer	to read
invertir	to invest	legumbres (las)	pulses

lejos de	far from	manta (la)	blanket
lenguaje (el)	language	mantel (el)	tablecloth
lentejas (las)	lentils	mantequilla (la)	butter
letra (la)	letter	manzana (la)	apple
levantarse	to get up	mañana	tomorrow
libre	free	mañana (la)	morning
librería (la)	book shop	máquinilla de	shaving razor
libreta (la)	passbook	afeitar (la)	
libro (el)	book	mar (el/la)	sea
licenciado/a	postgraduate	marcador (el)	scoreboard
ligero/a	light	marido(el)/mujer	husband/wife
límite de	speed limit	(la)	
velocidad (el)		mariposa (la)	butterfly
limpia-parabrisas	windscreen	marisco (el)	sea food
(el)	wiper	marrón	brown
limpio/a	clean	martes (el)	Tuesday
línea (la)	line	matemáticas (las)	Mathematics
líneas aéreas	airlines	matrimonio (el)	couple (married)
(las)		mayor	elderly/ older
liso/a	straight/plain	mechero (el)/	lighter
litera (la)	berth	encendedor (el)	
llamar	to call	medias (las)	stockings/ tights
llamarse	to call oneself	medicina (la)	medicine
llano/a	plain	médico/a	doctor
llegada (la)	arrival	medios de	mass media
llegar	to arrive/ to reach	comunicación (los)	
llegar a tener	to achieve	mejicano/a	Mexican
llevar	to take/ to bring	melocotón (el)	peach
llorar	to cry	melón (el)	melon
llover	to rain	menudo/a	small framed
locutor/a	newsreader /	mercado (el)	market
	announcer	mercería (la)	hosiery shop
luego	later	merendar	to have tea
lunes (el)	Monday	mermelada (la)	jam
		mesa (la)	table
M		meter	to put in
		metro (el)	metro/
madera (la)	wood		underground
madre (la)	mother	micrófono (el)	microphone
maestro/a	teacher	miel (la)	honey
maleta (la)	suitcase	miércoles (el)	Wednesday
malo/a	bad	mismo/a	same
mano (la)	hand		

mochila (la)	rucksack/ backpack	normalmente	normally
moderno/a	modern	norte (el)	north
momento	moment	notas (las)	marks
moneda (la)	coin	novio/a	bridegroom/ bride boyfriend/ girlfriend
montaña (la)	mountain		
monte (el)	mount	nube (la)	cloud
moreno/a	dark haired	nublado	cloudy
mosca (la)	fly	número (el)	number
mosquito (el)	mosquito	nunca	never
moto (la)	motorcycle		
mucho	lot	**O**	
muelle (el)	wharf/docks	obra (la)	play
multa (la)	fine	ocupado/a	busy
museo (el)	museum	oeste (el)	west
músico/a	musician	oficina (la)	office
muslo (el)	thigh	oficina de correos (la)	post office
muy	very		
		oír	to hear
N		ojo (el)	eye
nacer	to be born	ola (la)	wave
nacionalidad (la)	nationality	oler	to smell
nada	nothing	olla (la)	vessel
nadar	to swim	oreja (la)	ear
naranja (la)	orange	orilla (la)	shore
nariz (la)	nose	oro (el)	gold
nata (la)	cream	orquesta (la)	orchestra
natación (la)	swimming	oscuro/a	dark
navegar	to sail	otoño (el)	autumn
navidad (la)	Christmas	ovalado/a	oval
necesitar	to need	oveja (la)	sheep
negociante	businessman		
negro/a	black	**P**	
nepalí	Nepalese	padre (el)	father
nervioso/a	nervous	pagar	to pay
neumático (el)	tyre	país	country
nevar	to snow	paisaje (el)	landscape
nevera (la)	refrigerator	pájaro (el)	bird
niebla (la)	fog	pakistaní	Pakistani
niño/a	child	palabra (la)	word
noche (la)	night	palacio (el)	palace
nombre (el)	name	pan (el)	bread

160

panadero/a	baker	pensión (la)	boarding house
pantalla (la)	screen	pequeño/a	small
pantalones (los)	trousers	pera (la)	pear
papel (el)	paper	perder	to lose
papelería (la)	stationary shop	perdonar	to excuse
paquete (el)	packet	perfumería (la)	cosmetic shop
parada de autobuses (la)	bus stop	periódico (el)	newspaper
		periodista (el, la)	journalist
parada de taxis (la)	taxi stand	permiso de conducir (el)	driving license
paraguas (el)	umbrella	pero	but
paraguayo/a	Paraguayan	perro/a	dog
parar	stop	persona (la)	person
pareja (la)	partner	pertenecer	to belong
parlamento (el)	parliament	peruano / a	Peruvian
parque (el)	park	pesado/a	heavy
partidos políticos (los)	political parties	pescado (el)	fish
		pianista (el, la)	pianist
pasajero/a	passenger	picadora (la)	chopper
pasaporte (el)	passport	picante	spicy
pasar	to pass	picar (algo)	to have a bite
pasar las vacaciones	to spend the vacations	pico (el)	peak
		pie (el)	foot
pasear	to take a walk	piel (la)	skin
pasillo (el)	passage/ corridor	pierna (la)	leg
pasta de dientes (la)	toothpaste	píldora (la)	pill
		piloto	pilot
pastel (el)	cake	pimienta (la)	pepper
pastelería (la)	pastry shop	pimiento (el)	capsicum
pastilla (la)	tablet/ pill	pintor / a	painter
patata (la)	potato	piña (la)	pineapple
peaje (el)	toll	pipa (la)	pipe
pecoso/a	freckled	piscina (la)	swimming pool
peine (el)	comb	piso (el)	flat
pelar	to peel	planchar	to iron
película (la)	film	plano (el)	street map
pelirrojo/a	red haired	planta (la)	plant
pelo (el)	hair	plástico (el)	plastic
peluquería (la)	barber's shop, hair dresser shop	plata (la)	silver
		plátano (el)	banana
		plato (el)	plate
pendientes (los)	earrings	playa (la)	beach

161

plaza (la)	square	publicidad (la)	advertising/
plaza de toros (la)	bullring		publicity
poder	to be able to	pueblo (el)	village
poeta / poetisa	poet/ poetess	puerta (la)	door
polideportivo (el)	sports centre	puerta de	boarding gate
política (la)	politics	embarque (la)	
pollo (el)	chicken	puerto (el)	port
poner	to put	pues	well
por cierto	by the way	pulmones (los)	lungs
por qué	why	pulsera (la)	bangle
por supuesto	of course	puré (el)	puré
porque	because		
portería (la)	goal line	**Q**	
portero/a	concierge/ gatekeeper	quedar con	to make an appointment
portero	goalkeeper	quedar en	to agree on/to
portugués	Portuguese	quedarse	to stay/ remain
postre (el)	dessert	quedarse (con)	to keep some-
precio (el)	price	algo	thing
pregunta (la)	question	querer	to want
preguntar por	to ask about/ to enquire	queso (el)	cheese
		química (la)	Chemistry
prensa (la)	press	quiosco (el)	newsstand
preocupado/a	worried	quitar	to take off/ to
preparar	to prepare		remove
presentador/a	announcer		
presentar	to introduce	**R**	
primavera (la)	spring		
primo/a	cousin	radio (la)	radio
príncipe (el)/	prince/princess	rama (la)	branch
princesa (la)		rápido/a	quick
probador (el)	trial room	raqueta (la)	racket
probar	to taste	raro/a	strange/ weird
probarse	to try on	rato (el)	(a) while
problema (el)	problem	rayo (el)	lightning
profesión (la)	profession	rebajas (las)	sales
profesor (el)	professor/ teacher	rebanada (la)	slice
		recepcionista	receptionist
programa (el)	programme	(el, la)	
propina (la)	tip	recibidor (el)	hall/ lobby
próximo estreno (el)	next release	recibo (el)	receipt
		recoger	to collect
psiquiatra (el, la)	psychiatrist		

recoger a alguien	to pick some-one up	salón de belleza (el)	beauty parlour
recto/a	straight	sandalias (las)	sandals
red (la)	net	sandía (la)	watermelon
redondo/a	round	sartén (la)	frying pan
refresco (el)	cold drink	satisfecho/a	satisfied
regalo (el)	gift	seco/a	dry
reir	to laugh	seda (la)	silk
reloj (el)	watch	seguir	to follow
repetir	to repeat	seguridad social (la)	social security
reportaje (el)	report		
reservar	to reserve	sello (el)	stamp
resfriado (el)	cold	sentarse	to sit down
revisor (el)	ticket inspector	sentir	to feel
revista (la)	magazine	ser	to be
rey (el)/ reina (la)	king/ queen	serio/a	serious
río (el)	river	servicio militar(el)	military service
rizado/a	curly	servilleta (la)	napkin
roca (la)	rock	siempre	always
rodilla (la)	knee	significado (el)	meaning
rojo/a	red	silla (la)	chair
rosa	pink/ rose	sillón (el)	armchair
rubio/a	blonde	simpático/a	kind/ nice
rueda (la)	wheel	sindicato (el)	trade union
ruidoso/a	noisy	sirena (la)	siren/ alarm
ruso/a	Russian	sitio (el)	place
		sobre	on
S		sobre (el)	envelope
		sobrino/a	nephew/niece
sábado (el)	Saturday	socialista (el/ la)	socialist
sábana (la)	sheet	sofá (el)	sofa
saber	to know	sol (el)	sun
sabroso/a	tasty	solo/a	alone
sacar	to take out	soltero/a	unmarried/ single
sacar dinero	to withdraw	sopa (la)	soup
sal (la)	salt	soso/a	tasteless
sala (la)	room	suave	gentle/ soft
sala de estar	living room	sucio/a	dirty
salado/a	salty	suegro/a	father/mother in law
salida (la)	departure/ exit		
salir	to go out/ to leave	supermercado (el)	supermarket
salón (el)	drawing room/ living room		

suplemento (el)	supplement/ surcharge	terraza (la)	terrace
sur (el)	south	tesis (la)	thesis
suspender	to fail	tiempo (el)	weather/time
		tienda (la)	shop
T		tierra (la)	land
		tijeras (las)	scissors
tabaco (el)	tobacco	tío/a	uncle/aunt
tacaño/a	miserly	titulares (los)	headlines
talla (la)	size	tobillo (el)	ankle
también	also	tocar	to touch
tapas (las)	snacks	tomar	to take
taquilla (la)	box office	tomar copas	to have drinks
tarde	late	tomar el aperitivo	to have an aperitif
tarde (la)	evening		
tarjeta (la)	card	tomar el sol	to sunbathe
tarjeta de banco (la)	bank card	tomate (el)	tomato
		tonto/a	stupid, silly
tarjeta de crédito (la)	credit card	torero/a	bullfighter
		tormenta (la)	storm
taza (la)	cup	toro (el)	bull
té (el)	tea	tostado/a	toast
teatro (el)	theatre	tostar	to toast
tebeo (el)	comic/ cartoon	trabajar	to work
técnico/a	technician	trabajar la tierra	to till the land
teléfono (el)	telephone	traducir	to translate
televisión (la)	television	traer	to bring
temperatura (la)	temperature	traje (el)	suit
templado/a	lukewarm	tranquilo/a	quiet / calm
tenedor (el)	fork	triangular	triangular
tener	to have	triste	sad
tener calor	to be hot	tronco (el)	trunk (of a tree, body)
tener frío	to be cold		
tener ganas de	to desire	turista (el / la)	tourist
tener hambre	to be hungry		
tener prisa	to be in a hurry	**U**	
tener razón	to be right	último/a	last
tener sed	to be thirsty	ultramarinos (el)	grocery shop
tener sueño	to be sleepy	universidad (la)	university
tenis (el)	tennis	urgencias	emergency
terminal (la)	terminal	uruguayo/a	Uruguayan
termómetro (el)	thermometer	uva (la)	grape
ternera (la)	beef		

V

vaca (la)	cow
vacaciones (las)	vacations
valle (el)	valley
varios	several
vaso (el)	glass
vecino/a	neighbour
venda (la)	bandage
vendedor de prensa	newspaper vendor
venezolano/a	Venezuelan
venir	to come from
ventana (la)	window
ventilador (el)	fan
ver	to see
verano (el)	summer
verde	green
verdura (la)	vegetable
vestido (el)	dress
vía (la)	rail
viajar	to travel
viajero/a	traveller
vida (la)	life
viejo/a	old
viento (el)	wind
viernes (el)	Friday
vinagre (el)	vinegar
vino (el)	wine
violeta	violet
violinista (el, la)	violinist
viudo/a	widower/ widow
vivir	to live
volante (el)	steering wheel
volver	to return/ to come back
votar	to vote
vuelo (el)	flight

Y

y	and
yerno (el)/ nuera (la)	son/daughter in law
yogur (el)	yogurt

Z

zapatillas (las)	sport shoes
zapatos (los)	shoes
zumo (el)	fruit juice

(English to Spanish)

A

above	encima
accelerator	acelerador (el)
action	acción (la)
actor	actor (el)
actress	actriz (la)
adult	adulto/a
address	dirección (la)
advertisement	anuncio (el)
advertising/ publicity	publicidad (la)
after	después de
age	edad (la)
air	aire (el)
air hostess/ steward	azafata / o
airlines	líneas aéreas (las)
airport	aeropuerto (el)
almost	casi
alone	solo/a
also	también
always	siempre
ambulance	ambulancia (el)
American	americano / a
and	y
ankle	tobillo (el)
announcer	presentador/a
antenna	antena (la)
apartment	apartamento (el)
apple	manzana (la)
architect	arquitecto / a
Argentinean	argentino / a
arm	brazo (el)
armchair	sillón (el)
arrival	llegada (la)
article	artículo (el)
artist	artista (el / la)
athletics	atletismo (el)
aubergine/ brinjal	berenjena (la)

automatic teller machine	cajero autómatico (el)
autumn	otoño (el)
(a) while	rato (el)

B

back	espalda (la)
bad	malo/a
bag/ handbag	bolso (el)
baker	panadero/a
balcony	balcón (el)
ball	balón (el)/pelota (la)
banana	plátano (el)
bandage	venda (la)
bangle	pulsera (la)
bank card	tarjeta de banco (la)
bank/ bench	banco (el)
barber's shop/ hair dresser shop	peluquería (la)
basketball	baloncesto (el)
bathroom	cuarto de baño(el)
bathtub	bañera (la)
beach	playa (la)
battery	batería (la)/pila (la)
beans	judías (las)
beard	barba (la)
beautiful	bonito/a
beautiful/ handsome/ pretty	guapo/a
beauty parlour	salón de belleza (el)
because	porque
bed	cama (la)
bedroom	dormitorio (el)
beef	ternera (la)
beer	cerveza (la)

166

behind	detrás (de)	brother/ sister	hermano/a
belt	cinturón (el)	brother/ sister in law	cuñado/a
berth	litera (la)	brown	marrón
bicycle	bicicleta (la)	brush	cepillo (el)
big	grande	building	edificio (el)
bill	cuenta (la)	bull	toro (el)
billboard	cartelera (la)	bullfight	corrida (la)
bird	pájaro (el)	bullfighter	torero/a
bitter	amargo / a	bullring	plaza de toros (la)
black	negro/a	bus	autobús (el)
blanket	manta (la)	bus stop	parada de autobuses (la)
blinker/ indicator	intermitente (el)	bus terminal	estación de autobuses (la)
blonde	rubio/a	businessman	negociante
blouse	blusa (la)	busy	ocupado/a
blue	azul	but	pero
boarding gate	puerta de embarque (la)	butter	mantequilla (la)
boarding house	pensión (la)	butterfly	mariposa (la)
		by the way	por cierto
Bolivian	boliviano/a		
book	libro (el)		
book shop	librería (la)	**C**	
border (of the road)	arcén (el)	cabbage	col (la)
boring	aburrido/a	cabin	cabina (la)
bottle	botella (la)	cake	pastel (el)
bowl	cuenco (el)	can	bote (el)
box office	taquilla (la)	cape	cabo (el)
box, cash counter	caja (la)	capsicum	pimiento (el)
boyfriend/ girlfriend	novio/a	car	coche (el)
		card	tarjeta (la)
brake	freno (el)	carpenter	carpintero / a
branch	rama (la)	carpet	alfombra (la)
Brazilian	brasileño/a	cart	carro (el)
bread	pan (el)	cash/ money	dinero (el)
breakfast	desayuno (el)	cashier	cajero (el)
bridegroom/ bride	novio/a	casserole/ saucepan	cacerola (la)
broth/ clear soup	caldo (el)	castle	castillo (el)
		cat	gato/a
		cathedral	catedral (la)
		cauliflower	coliflor (la)

centre	centro (el)	comic/ cartoon	tebeo (el)
chair	silla (la)	communist	comunista (el / la)
chance	casualidad (la)	company	empresa (la)
characteristic	característica (la)	concert	concierto (el)
chauffeur	chófer	concierge/	portero/a
cheap	barato/a	gatekeeper	
cheese	queso (el)	consulting	consulta (la)
chemist shop	farmacia (la)	chamber	
Chemistry	química (la)	conservative	conservador/a
cherry	cereza (la)	cooked	cocido/a
chick peas	garbanzos (los)	corner	esquina (la)
chicken	pollo (el)	cosmetic shop	perfumería (la)
child	niño/a	cotton	algodón (el)
Chilean	chileno / a	council of	consejo de
chilli	guindilla (la)	ministers	ministros (el)
Chinese	chino / a	country side	campo (el)
chopper	picadora (la)	couple	matrimonio (el)
christmas	navidades (las)	(married)	
church	iglesia (la)	course	curso (el)
cinema	cine (el)	court	cancha (la)/ pista (la)
civil status	estado civil (el)	cousin	primo/a
class	clase (la)	cow	vaca (la)
classic	clásico/a	crane	grúa (la)
clean	limpio/a	cream	nata (la)
clear	claro/a	credit card	tarjeta de crdito(la)
clinic	clínica (la)	Cuban	cubano / a
clothes	ropa (la)	cup	taza (la)
cloud	nube (la)	cup	copa (la)
cloudy	nublado	cupboard/	armario (el)
coast	costa (la)	wardrobe	
coat	abrigo (el)	curly	rizado/a
cock	gallo (el)	current	cuenta corriente
coffee	café (el)	account	(la)
coin	moneda (la)	curtain	cortina (la)
cold	resfriado (el)/frío/a	customs	aduana (la)
cold drink	refresco (el)	cutlery	cubiertos (los)
colleague	compañero/a		
Colombian	colombiano / a	**D**	
colony/	barrio (el)	dark	oscuro/a
neighbourhood		dark haired	moreno/a
comb	peine (el)	date	fecha (la)
comfortable	cómodo/a	daughter in law	nuera (la)

168

day	día (el)
deck	cubierta (la)
degree	grado (el)
departmental	grandes
store	almacenes (los)
departure/ exit	salida (la)
designer	diseñador/a
dessert	postre (el)
destination	destino (el)
/ destiny	
detergent/	detergente (el)
washing powder	
dictionary	diccionario (el)
diesel oil	gasóleo (el)
difficult	difícil
dining room	comedor (el)
dinner	cena (la)
diploma	diploma (el)
dirty	sucio/a
discothèque	discoteca (la)
discount	descuento (el)
dishwasher	lavaplatos (el)
divorced	divorciado/a
dock	dársena (la)
docks	muelle (el)
doctor	doctor/a
doctor	médico/a
dog	perro/a
donkey	burro /a
door	puerta (la)
double room	habitación doble (la)
down	abajo
drawing room,	salón (el)
living room	
dress	vestido (el)
driver	conductor / a
driving license	permiso de conducir (el)
drums	batería (la)
dry	seco/a

E

ear	oreja (la)
earrings	pendientes (los)
east	este
easy	fácil
education	educación (la)/ enseñanza (la)
egg	huevo (el)
elbow	codo (el)
elderly, older	mayor
elections	elecciones (las)
electrician	electricista (el / la)
elegant	elegante
emergency	urgencias
employee	empleado/a
end	final (el)
engineer	ingeniero / a
English	inglés / a
enough	bastante
envelope	sobre (el)
envious	envidioso/a
evening	tarde (la)
exam	examen (el)
expensive	caro/a
eye	ojo (el)

F

factory	fábrica (la)
family	familia (la)
fan	ventilador (el)
far (from)	lejos (de)
farmer	agricultor/a
fat	gordo/a
father	padre (el)
father/mother in law	suegro/a
feel	sentir
film	película (la)
fine	multa (la)
finger	dedo (el)
fish	pescado (el)

flat	piso (el)	graduate	diplomado/a
flatmate	compañero/a de piso	grandfather/ grandmother	abuelo/a
flight	vuelo (el)	grape	uva (la)
flour	harina (la)	grass	hierba (la)
flower	flor (la)	great	estupendo/a
fly	mosca (la)	green	verde
fog	niebla (la)	grey	gris
food mixer	batidora (la)	grocery shop	ultramarinos (el)
foot	pie (el)	Guatemalan	guatemalteco / a
football	fútbol (el)	guide	guía
foreign/ abroad	extranjero/a	guitar	guitarra (la)
fork	tenedor (el)	gulf	golfo (el)
freckled	pecoso/a	gymnastics	gimnasia (la)
free	libre		
French	francés/a	**H**	
fresh	fresco/a		
Friday	viernes (el)	hair	pelo (el)
friend	amigo/a	hall/lobby	recibidor (el)
fruit	fruta (la)	ham	jamón (el)
fruit juice	zumo (el)	hamlet	aldea (la)
frying pan	sartén (la)	hand	mano (la)
function/ show	función (la)	handbrake	freno de mano (el)
funny	divertido/a	happy	contento/a/ feliz
		hard pork sausage	chorizo (el)
G		head	cabeza (la)
garage	garaje (el)	headlines	titulares (los)
garlic	ajo (el)	heart	corazón (el)
gel	gel (el)	heavy	pesado/a
generous	generoso/a	hen	gallina (la)
gentle, soft	suave	here	aquí
German	alemán / a	hill	colina (la)
gift	regalo (el)	history/ story	historia (la)
glass	vaso (el)	holiday	día festivo (el)
glass	copa (la)	honey	miel (la)
glove compartment	guantera (la)	horrible	horrible
goal line	portería (la)	horse	caballo (el)
goalkeeper	portero	hosiery shop	mercería (la)
gold	oro (el)	hospital	hospital (el)
good	bueno/a	host/hostess	anfitrión/a (el/la)
government employee	funcionario/a	hot	caliente
		housewife / house husband	ama/o de casa

husband /wife	marido(el) /mujer (la)	king/ queen	rey (el)/ reina (la)
hygiene	higiene (la)	kitchen	cocina (la)
		knee	rodilla (la)
		knife	cuchillo (el)

I

ice	hielo (el)
ice cream	helado (el)
ideal	ideal
ill/ sick	enfermo/a
importance	importancia (la)
in	en
in front (of)	enfrente (de)
in front of	delante de
Indian	indio / a
industry	industria (la)
infusion	infusión (la)
injection	inyección (la)
injured	herido/a
injury	herida
institute	instituto (el)
intelligent	inteligente
interesting	interesante
interior decorator	decorador / a
island	isla (la)
Italian	italiano / a

J

jacket	chaqueta (la)
jam	mermelada (la)
Japanese	japonés/a
jealous	celoso/a
journalist	periodista (el, la)
judo	judo (el)
jug	jarra (la)
justice	justicia (la)

K

kidney beans	alubias (las)
kind	amable
kind/ nice	simpático/a

L

lake	lago (el)
lamb, mutton	cordero (el)
lamp	lámpara (la)
lamppost	farola (la)
land	tierra (la)
landscape	paisaje (el)
language	idioma (el)/ lengua (la)
last	último/a
later	luego
laundry service	lavandería (la)
lawyer	abogado/a
leaf/ sheet of paper	hoja (la)
leather	cuero (el)
left	izquierda
left-luggage office	consigna (la)
leg	pierna (la)
lentils	lentejas (las)
letter/ menu	carta (la)
lettuce	lechuga (la)
life	vida (la)
lift/ elevator	ascensor (el)
light	ligero/a claro/a
lighter	mechero (el)/ encendedor (el)
lightning	rayo (el)
line	línea (la)
living room	sala de estar
lobster	langosta (la)
long	largo/a
loudspeaker	altavoz (el)
(a) lot	mucho
lugagge registration	facturación de equipajes (la)

171

luggage	equipaje (el)	mother	madre (la)
lukewarm	templado/a	motorcycle	moto (la)
lunch	comida (la)	motorway/	autopista (la)
lunchbox	fiambrera (la)	highway	
lungs	pulmones (los)	mount	monte (el)
		mountain	montaña (la)
M		mountain range	cordillera (la)
magazine	revista (la)	mouth	boca (la)
man	hombre (el)	museum	museo (el)
manager	empresario/a	musician	músico/a
manager/ principal / director	director/a	**N**	
market	mercado (el)	name	nombre (el)
marks	notas (las)	napkin	servilleta (la)
married	casado/a	narrow	estrecho/a
mason	albañil	nationality	nacionalidad (la)
mass media	medios de comunicación (los)	near	cerca (de)
		neck	cuello (el)
		necklace	collar (el)
match-stick	cerilla (la)	neighbour	vecino/a
Mathematics	matemáticas (las)	Nepalese	nepalí
mattress	colchón (el)	nephew/niece	sobrino/a
meaning	significado (el)	nervous	nervioso/a
meat	carne (la)	net	red (la)
meat shop	carnicería (la)	never	nunca
medicine	medicina (la)	newscast	informativo (el)
melon	melón (el)	newscaster	locutor/a
metro/ underground	metro (el)	newspaper	periódico (el)
		newspaper vendor	vendedor de prensa
Mexican	mejicano/a	newsstand	quiosco (el)
microphone	micrófono (el)	night	noche (la)
midday meal	almuerzo (el)	noisy	ruidoso/a
military service	servicio militar(el)	normally	normalmente
milk	leche (la)	north	norte (el)
mirror	espejo (el)	nose	nariz (la)
miserly	tacaño/a	notebook	cuaderno (el)
modern	moderno/a	nothing	nada
moment	momento	number	número (el)
Monday	lunes (el)	nurse	enfermero/a
morning	mañana (la)		
mosquito	mosquito (el)		

O

of course	por supuesto
office	oficina (la)
oil	aceite (el)
old/ancient	antiguo/a
old	viejo/a
old man/ woman	anciano/a
olive	aceituna (la)
on	sobre
onion	cebolla (la)
orange	naranja (la)
orchestra	orquesta (la)
oval	ovalado/a
oven	horno (el)

P

packet	paquete (el)
pain	dolor (el)
painter	pintor / a
painting	cuadro (el)
Pakistani	pakistaní
palace	palacio (el)
paper	papel (el) / asignatura (la)
Paraguayan	paraguayo/a
park	parque (el)
parking	aparcamiento (el)
parliament	parlamento (el)
partner	pareja (la)
party	fiesta (la)
passage/ corridor	pasillo (el)
passbook	libreta (la)
passenger	pasajero/a
passport	pasaporte (el)
passport control	control de pasaportes (el)
pastry shop	pastelería (la)
pavement	acera (la)
pea	guisante (el)
peach	melocotón (el)

peak	pico (el)
pear	pera (la)
pencil	lápiz (el)
people	gente (la)
pepper	pimienta (la)
person	persona (la)
Peruvian	peruano / a
petrol	gasolina (la)
petrol station	gasolinera (la)
PhD	doctorado/a
photo	foto (la)
Physics	física (la)
pianist	pianista (el, la)
picture/ illustration	ilustración (la)
pig/ pork	cerdo (el)
pill	píldora (la)
pillow	almohada (la)
pilot	piloto
pineapple	piña (la)
pink	rosa
pipe	pipa (la)
pitch/ soccer field	campo de fútbol (el)
place	sitio (el)
plain	llano/a
plane	avión (el)
plant	planta (la)
plaster	escayola (la)
plastic	plástico (el)
plate	plato (el)
platform	andén (el)
play	obra (la)
pleasant	agradable
plug	enchufe (el)
plumber	fontanero / o
poet/ poetess	poeta / poetisa
polite	amable
political parties	partidos políticos (los)
politics	política (la)
port	puerto (el)

173

Portuguese	portugués/a	red haired	pelirrojo/a
post office	correos/ oficina de correos (la)	referee	árbitro (el)
		refrigerator	nevera (la)
postgraduate	licenciado/a	release	próximo estreno (el)
postman	cartero / a		
potato	patata (la)	report	informe (el)/ reportaje (el)
prawn	gamba (la)		
press	prensa (la)	right	derecha
price	precio (el)	ring	anillo (el)
prince / princess	príncipe (el)/ princesa (la)	river	río (el)
		road	carretera (la)
printed (material or cloth)	estampado/a	rock	roca (la)
		room	habitación (la)
problem	problema (el)	round	redondo/a
profession	profesión (la)	row/ line	fila (la)
professor	catedrático / a	rucksack/ backpack	mochila (la)
professor/ teacher	profesor (el)	rude/ indecent	grosero/a
programme	programa (el)	Russian	ruso/a
psychiatrist	psiquiatra (el, la)		
pulses	legumbres (las)	**S**	
pumpkin	calabaza (la)	sad	triste
pupil	alumno/a	safe	cajafuerte (la)
puré	puré (el)	salad	ensalada (la)
		salami	chorizo (el)
Q		sales	rebajas (las)
question	pregunta (la)	salt	sal (la)
queue	cola (la)	salty	salado/a
quick	rápido/a	same	mismo/a
quiet/ calm	tranquilo/a	sand	arena (la)
		sandals	sandalias (las)
R		sandwich	bocadillo (el)
racket	raqueta (la)	satisfied	satisfecho/a
radio	radio (la)	Saturday	sábado (el)
rail	vía (la)	sausage	embutido (el)
railway station	estación de trenes (la)	savings account	cuenta de ahorro (la)
raw	crudo/a	senator	diputado (el)/ senador (el)
receipt	recibo (el)		
receptionist	recepcionista (el, la)	scale	escala (la)
		scenery	decorado/a
red	rojo/a	school	escuela (la), colegio (el)

174

scientist	científico / a	sleeping wagon	coche cama (el)
scissors	tijeras (las)	slice	rebanada (la)
scoreboard	marcador (el)	slope	ladera (la)
screen	pantalla (la)	small	pequeño/a
sea	mar (el/la)	small framed	menudo/a
season of the year	estación del año (la)	snacks	tapas (las)
seat	asiento (el)/ butaca (la)	soap	jabón (el)
		social security	seguridad social (la)
serious	serio/a		
serving dish/ fountain	fuente (la)	socialist	socialista (el, la)
		socks	calcetines (los)
several	varios	sofa	sofá (el)
shampoo	champú (el)	someone	alguien
shares	acción (la)	something	algo
shaving razor	mquinilla de afeitar (la)	son in law	yerno (el)
		son/ daughter	hijo/a
sheep	oveja (la)	soup	sopa (la)
sheet	sábana (la)	sour	agrio (el)
shelf	estantería (la)	south	sur (el)
shellfish	marisco (el)	Spanish	español / a
ship	barco (el)	spectator	espectador/a
shoes	zapatos (los)	speed limit	límite de velocidad (el)
shop	tienda (la)		
shop assistant	dependiente (el / la)	spicy	picante
		spinach	espinacas (las)
shop window	escaparate (el)	sponge	esponja (la)
shopping	compras (las)	spoon	cuchara (la)
shore	orilla (la)	sport	deporte (el)
short	bajo/a corto/a	sport shoes	zapatillas (las)
		sports centre	polideportivo (el)
shoulder	hombro (el)	sportsman	deportista (el / la)
shower	ducha (la)	sporty	deportivo / a
silk	seda (la)	spring	primavera (la)
silver	plata (la)	square	cuadrado/a
singer	cantante (el / la)	square	plaza (la)
single room	habitación sencilla (la)	stairs	escaleras (las)
		stamp	sello (el)
sink	fregadero (el)	stationary shop	papelería (la)
siren/ alarm	sirena (la)		
skin	piel (la)	steering wheel	volante (el)
skinny	flaco/a	stock market/ plastic or cloth carry bag	bolsa (la)
skirt	falda (la)		

175

stockings, tights	medias (las)	tap	grifo (el)
store where cleaning materials are sold	droguería (la)	tasteless	soso/a
		tasty	sabroso/a
		taxi stand	parada de taxis(la)
		tea	té (el)
stomach	estómago (el)	teacher	maestro/a
stop	parar	team	equipo (el)
storm	tormenta (la)	technician	técnico/a
straight	recto/a	telephone	teléfono (el)
straight, plain	liso/a	telephone booth	cabina de teléfonos (la)
strange	extraño/a	television	televisión (la)
strange, weird	raro/a	temperature	temperatura (la)
strawberry	fresa (la)	tennis	tenis (el)
street	calle (la)	terminal	terminal (la)
street map	plano (el)	terrace	terraza (la)
stretcher	camilla (la)	thanks	gracias (las)
strike	huelga (la)	theatre	teatro (el)
strong	fuerte	then	entonces
student	estudiante (el / la)	there	allí
stupid/ silly	tonto/a	thermometer	termómetro (el)
subject	asignatura (la)	thesis	tesis (la)
sugar	azúcar (el)	thigh	muslo (el)
suit	traje (el)	thin	delgado/a
suitcase	maleta (la)	thing	cosa (la)
summer	verano (el)	throat	garganta (la)
sun	sol (el)	Thursday	jueves (el)
Sunday	domingo (el)	ticket	billete (el)
supermarket	supermercado (el)	ticket inspector	revisor (el)
supplement	suplemento (el)	tiecorbata (la)	
surname	apellido (el)	time/ hour	hora (la)
sweet	dulce	timetable	horario (el)
sweater	jersei (el)	tinlata (la)	
swimming	natación (la)	tippropina (la)	
swimming pool	piscina (la)	tired	cansado/a
syrup	jarabe (el)	to attend	atender
		to achieve	llegar a tener
T		to agree on/to	quedar en
t-shirt	camiseta (la)	to answer	contestar
table	mesa (la)	to arrive, reach	llegar
tablecloth	mantel (el)		
tablet, pill	pastilla (la)	to ask about, to enquire	preguntar por
tall	alto/a		

to bathe	bañarse	to cross	cruzar
to be	estar/ser	to cry	llorar
to be able to	poder	to rain	llover
to be born	nacer	to cut	cortar
to be cold	tener frío	to dance	bailar
to be glad	estar contento	to decide	decidir
to be happy	estar alegre	to depend	depender
to be hot	tener calor	to deposit	ingresar dinero
to be hungry	tener hambre	money	
to be in a hurry	tener prisa	to describe	describir
to be in bed	estar acostado	to desire	desear
to be interested	interesarse	to want	querer
about/in	por/en	to desire	tener ganas de
to be moving	estar moviédose	to do	hacer
to be right	tener razón	to eat	comer
to be sad	estar triste	to embark	embarcar
to be sitting down	estar sentado	to enjoy, to	divertirse
to be sleepy	tener sueño	amuse oneself	
to be standing	estar de pie	to enter	entrar
(up)		to equalize, to	empatar
to be thirsty	tener sed	draw, to tie	
to be walking	estar andando	to excuse	perdonar
to become	hacerse	to explain	explicar
to become cold	enfriarse	to fail	suspender
to begin/	empezar	to find	encontrar
to start		to follow	seguir
to belong	pertenecer	to fry	freir
to boil	hervir	to function	funcionar
to bring	traer	to get down	bajar
to buy	comprar	to get undressed	desnudarse,
to call	llamar		desvestirse
to call oneself	llamarse	to get up	levantarse
to cancel	cancelar	to give	dar
to catch	coger	to give up	dejar de
to chat	charlar	something	
to clean	lavar	to go	ir
to close	cerrar	to go out,	salir
to collect	recoger	to leave	
to come from	venir	to go to bed	acostarse
to confirm	confirmar	to go with	acompañar
to consult	consultar	to hail	granizar
to converse	conversar	to have	tener
to count	contar	to have a bite	picar (algo)

to have a drink	tomar copas	to realise	darse cuenta de
to have a job	dedicarse	to rent	alquilar
to have an aperitif	tomar el aperitivo	to repeat	repetir
		to reserve	reservar
to have breakfast	desayunar	to rest	descansar
		to return, to come back	volver
to have dinner	cenar		
to have lunch	almorzar	to run	correr
to have tea	merendar	to sail	navegar
to have to, duty	deber	to save	ahorrar
to hear	oír	to say/ to tell	decir
to heat	calentar	to see	ver
to help	ayudar	to send	enviar
to interview	entrevistar	to shake hands	dar la mano
to introduce	presentar	to share	compartir
to invest	invertir	to shave	afeitarse
to iron	planchar	to sign	firmar
to keep something	quedarse (con) algo	to sit down	sentarse
		to ski	esquiar
to know	conocer / saber	to smell	oler
to laugh	reir(se)	to snow	nevar
to learn	aprender	to speak	hablar
to like	gustar	to spell out	deletrear
to listen	escuchar	to spend the vacations	pasar las vacaciones
to live	vivir		
to look for	buscar	to stay, remain	quedar quedarse
to lose	perder	to study	estudiar
to make an appointment	quedar con	to sunbathe	tomar el sol
		to swim	nadar
to meet	encontrarse	to take/ to have	tomar
to need	necesitar	to take off/ to remove	quitar
to open	abrir		
to pass	aprobar	to take out	sacar
to pass	pasar	to take/ to carry	llevar
to pay	pagar	to talk	conversar
to peel	pelar	to taste	probar
to pick someone up	recoger a alguien	to teach	enseñar
		to thank	agradecer
to play	jugar	to till the land	trabajar la tierra
to prepare	preparar	to toast	tostar
to put	poner	to translate	traducir
to put in	meter	to travel	viajar
to read	leer	to try on	probarse

178

to turn off the television	apagar la televisión	truck driver	camionero / a
to turn on the television	encender la televisión	trunk (of a tree, body)	tronco (el)
to understand	comprender	Tuesday	martes (el)
to vote	votar	tuna fish	atún (el)
to wait	esperar	tyre	neumtico (el)
to walk	pasear		
to want	querer	**U**	
to wash oneself	lavarse	ugly	feo/a
to win	ganar	umbrella	paraguas (el)
to withdraw	sacar dinero	umpleasant	desagradable
to work	trabajar	umpire, judge	juez/a
to write	escribir	uncomfortable	incómodo/a
to change	cambiar	uncle /aunt	tío/a
to cook	cocinar	university	universidad (la)
to touch	tocar	unkind	antipático/a
toast	tostado/a	unmarried/ single	soltero/a
tobacco	tabaco (el)	up	arriba
tobacco shop	estanco (el)	Uruguayan	uruguayo/a
today	hoy	usher	acomodador (el)
toilet	aseo (el)		
toll	peaje (el)	**V**	
tomato	tomate (el)		
tomorrow	mañana	vacations	vacaciones (las)
too much	demasiado	valley	valle (el)
toothbrush	cepillo de dientes (el)	vegetable	verdura (la)
		Venezuelan	venezolano/a
toothpaste	pasta de dientes (la)	very	muy
		vessel	olla (la)
tourist	turista (el / la)	village	pueblo (el)
'town	ciudad (la)	vinegar	vinagre (el)
track, lane	carril (el)	violet	violeta
trade union	sindicato (el)	violinist	violinista (el, la)
travel agency	agencia de viajes (la)		
		W	
travel bag	bolsa de viaje(la)		
traveller	viajero/a	waiter	camarero/a
tree	árbol (el)	wallet	cartera (la)
trial room	probador (el)	ward	sala (la)
triangular	triangular	washing machine	lavadora (la)
trousers	pantalones (los)		
truck	camión (el)	watch	reloj (el)

water	agua (el)	windscreen	limpia-parabrisas
watermelon	sandía (la)	wiper	(el)
wave	ola (la)	wine	vino (el)
weak	débil	winter	invierno (el)
weather	tiempo (el)	wood	madera (la)
Wednesday	mircoles (el)	woods	bosque (el)
week end	fin de semana	wool	lana (la)
	(el)	word	palabra (la)
welcome	bienvenido/a	worried	preocupado/a
well	pues	writer	escritor / a
well/ actually	bueno, bien		
west	oeste (el)	**Y**	
wharf	muelle (el)		
wheel	rueda (la)	year	año (el)
white	blanco/a	yellow	amarillo / a
why	por qué	yesterday	ayer
wide/ broad	ancho/a	yogurt	yogur (el)
widower/ widow	viudo/a	young	joven
wind	viento (el)	youth hostel	albergue (el)
window	ventana (la)		

ANSWER KEY

Unit 1

Exercise 1
a) es b) somos c) es d) son e) eres f) son g) soy

Exercise 2
Este niño habla español
Alberto tiene 25 años - Alberto habla español.
Las mujeres viven en Madrid - Los/esos hombres viven en Madrid.
Aquella chica es francesa - Las mujeres beben cerveza.
Esos/ Los hombres beben cerveza - Aquella chica tiene 25 años.
Los/ Esos gatos son blancos - Alberto es español.
Pablo y yo jugamos a baloncesto - Este niño es español.

Exercise 3
a) te llamas b) trabajan c) están estudiando d) vamos e) hace
f) habláis g) juego.

Exercise 4
a) Marta es de Bilbao. (Ella) Trabaja en Madrid.
b) ¿Vives en Delhi?
c) Los niños no están jugando en el jardín.

Unit 2

Exercise 1
a) es b) están c) Hay d) son e) están

Exercise 2
Las casas grandes
Los médicos buenos
La mujer alta y guapa
El reloj nuevo
Los edificios modernos
El vestido sucio

Las flores rojas

La camisa amarilla

Exercise 3

a)   donde, pocas/ muchas

b)   muchas, que

c)   quien

d)   bastante, pero

Exercise 4

a)   ¿Están las llaves sobre la mesa?/ ¿Las llaves están sobre la mesa?

b)   El hospital Santa Fe está al lado de la clínica de Ana. Es grande y muy bueno.

c)   Mi padre es alto y gordo. Lleva barba. Hoy lleva un abrigo negro y una chaqueta a cuadros.

d)   Hay muchos libros sobre mi mesa.

Unit 3

Exercise 1

a) alguien, nadie b) un, ninguno c) algo, nada d) alguna, ninguna e) otra, una f) un, ninguno.

Exercise 2

1) de 2) (a + el = al 3) de 4) a, en 5) por 6) por 7) sin / con 8) con / de 9) sobre

Exercise 3

1)   queda con 2) vuelven de 3) empiezo a 4) sales de 5) se preocupa por 6) me pongo a

Unit 4

Exercise 1

me levanto, desayuno, voy, trabajo, como, voy a cocinar, va a venir, voy a hacer, vamos a ir.

Exercise 2

12.45: es la una menos cuarto, 18.20: son las seis y veinte, 16.15: son las cuatro y cuarto, 20.35: son las nueve menos veinticinco, 21.30: son las nueve y media.

Exercise 3

a) se, se b) se c) me, me d) se, te e) nos, os

Unit 5

Exercise 1

a) has hecho, he llamado b) has estado, estuve c) fui, estuve, has hecho d) ha llovido e) fuimos, habéis ido.

Exercise 2

a) El miércoles pasado fui a una reunión muy importante, se estropeó el coche y llegué dos horas tarde

b) El sábado pasado fui de excursión con unos amigos, empezó a llover mucho, nos quedamos a dormir en un hotel de la carretera

c) La semana pasada no fui a trabajar, me quedé en casa para descansar, vino un amigo de India de visita, estuvimos todo el día hablando, no descansé nada

Exercise 3

El otro día/ El martes/ hace dos días mi marido y yo estuvimos cenando en casa de unos amigos

Esta semana/Ya/Esta mañana he comprado los regalos de navidad

Esta semana/Esta mañana Marcos ha hecho los deberes muy bien

Esta semana/Esta mañana mi marido y yo hemos ido al médico

El verano pasado Marcos fue a Roma de vacaciones

El otro día/El martes/Hace dos días me quedé en casa sola

Unit 6

Exercise 1

1. coge, sigue
2. tráigame, haga, siéntese
3. coged, bajad
4. haz, ven
5. comáis, cerrad, habléis

Exercise 2

a) María se las ha regalado b) Dáselos c) Cógela y échala a la comida d) Pruébatelo e) Tráigamelo g) Las he comprado en el mercado.

Exercise 3

a) le b) se c) se d) le, se e) le f) se g) le

183

Exercise 4

a) Dámelo en seguida porque lo necesito.
b) Tendré que quedármela para mirarla en casa.
c) Os las habéis comido todas / Te las has comido todas
d) ¿Por qué no los lees en clase?
e) Se las ponen cada domingo.

Unit 7

Exercise 1

a) viajaremos, b) vendrá, c) estudiaréis, d) cumplirá, e) ganarán,
f) invitarás.

Exercise 2

a) de, a, a, a, por, en
b) a, por, de
c) de, con, en, a, para
d) a, en, en, a.

Exercise 3

Si gano quinientas mil pesetas, compraremos un coche nuevo.
Si mi hermana saca buenas notas, la invitaré a cenar a un buen restaurante.
Si Carmen aprueba el carnet de conducir, su familia estará muy contenta.
Si compro un pastel de chocolate, invitaré a mis vecinos.

Unit 10

Exercise 1

a) tan, como, más, que
b) más, menos
c) tanto como, más
d) tan, como, más

Exercise 2

a) me quedan b) te parece c) nos gusta d) prefieres e) te gusta
f) me gusta g) me interesa h) nos molesta i) les divierte

Exercise 3

a) Me parece que va a llover
b) Me gustaría ir a París
c) Nos gustan los toros
d) Le gusta jugar a fútbol
e) Me parezco mucho a mi padre

Exercise 4

a) Me gustaría, pero he quedado con Julio

b) Me gustaría, pero estoy enferma

c) Me gustaría, pero no sé esquiar

d) Me gustaría, pero voy a India a ver el Taj Mahal

Exercise 5

a) ¿Te gustaría ir a España o prefieres quedarte aquí?

b) Los niños hacen mucho ruido. Si os molestan, podemos cerrar la puerta.

c) No deberías trabajar tanto. ¿Por qué no vamos de vacaciones a Manali?

Unit 11

Exercise 1

dormía, veía, oyó, fue, pasaba, encontró, volvió, siguió,

Exercise 2

a) trabajaba, iba, trabajo, estoy

b) se levantaba, está, se levanta

c) vivíamos, vivimos

d) era, hacía, puedo

e) tenías, te bañabas

Exercise 3

El martes pasado fui al dentista porque tenía mucho dolor de muelas.

El lunes pasado me quedé en casa porque estaba muy cansado.

La semana pasada Mario no fue al gimnasio porque le dolía mucho el pie.

El fin de semana pasado fuimos de excursión porque hacía muy buen tiempo.

Unit 14

Exercise 1

Jaime le preguntó por qué había llegado tan tarde y que dónde estaba y le dijo que fuera a estudiar enseguida y que el día siguiente hablaría con su profesora, esperaba que no suspendiera el examen.

Exercise 2

Juan preguntó a Miguel a qué hora iría a clase de inglés y Miguel le contestó que iría a las cinco.

Susana preguntó a Esteban qué tal era el restaurante 'Sancho', Esteban le contestó que era muy bueno y que siempre había mucha gente.

Gonzalo preguntó a Pepe si iba todos los días a la piscina y Pepe le contestó que no, que a veces iba a la playa.

Exercise 3
1. lloviera, iríamos
2. pongo, mancho
3. saldré, va
4. estudiases, sacarías
5. hubieras llegado, hubieses visto/ habrías visto

Unit 15

Exercise 1
a) llamase/ llamara b) acabe c) se había ido d) compremos e) estaba, llegó f) perdió, había regalado

Exercise 2
a) Es raro que Elisa no hable hindi a pesar de que hace quince anos que vive en Nueva Delhi.
b) Es normal que esperasen el resultado de los análisis, estaban preocupados
c) Es lógico que pague muchos impuestos, gana mucho dinero
d) Es increíble que hayan construído este edificio en dos meses
e) Es extraño que se haya cortado el pelo de nuevo, no le favorece nada

Exercise 3
a) esté b) acabemos c) trabaje d) fueseis e) trasladen f) terminéis g) sea

Exercise 4
a) Espero que el tren llegue pronto.
b) No hace falta que María venga a la fiesta.
c) Es increíble que Miguel gane tanto dinero.
d) Aunque haga frío saldremos a pasear.
e) Te he comprado este libro para que estudies.
f) Ojalá llueva pronto.